A Practical Guide to
TEEN BUSINESS
AND CYBERSECURITY

VOLUME 1

Cybersecurity and best practices,
Great Leadership Qualities, How to Write a
Press Release, Various Types of Investment
Capital, How to Avoid Phishing Attacks,
How to Defend Against Zero-Day Attacks,
and much more.

JAMES SCOTT

A Practical Guide to Teen Business and Cybersecurity – Volume 1

Copyright © 2016 James Scott

TABLE OF CONTENTS

INTRODUCTION

This book series isn't necessarily about financial endeavors, the love of money and power or pushing teens into any particular business-centric direction. Your children study history and mathematics without the motivating factor of being a professional historian or mathematician. This book of business and cybersecurity should be studied in the same manner. Education is about opening the student's mind to a universe of new possibilities and tearing down barriers. This book series stands as a testament that any and all information should be readily available to anyone regardless of age or geography when the student is ready to receive it, without systematic restriction by establishment topical guardians.

Standardized education has succeeded at nothing other than the dumbing down of our youth and inventing new inhibitors to information access. The brutal reality nowadays is that the education sector attracts teachers who teach because (in most cases) they cannot do, and these are the very people we allow 12+ years of access to our children. Ask your teen's 11th grade political science teacher what books he/she's published or what office within the legislative community they've held? I can virtually guarantee that they've published nothing and held no office that demanded real life usage of the content that they regurgitate onto a chalkboard in your child's classroom.

Let's face the facts; we've been bamboozled into believing that the school system knows best in matters of shaping and molding the developing minds of our children. We've been instructed by the institutional machine that our youth's mind and very being are nothing more than possessions of the state. This book series shatters the illusions and lies that school teachers, experts in nothing but recitation of words authored by someone else, are properly equipped to instruct your teen.

Take control of the education of your child. Give them the tools they'll need to succeed by instilling true and usable knowledge that will stand out amid the pretentious rhetoric they encounter daily. The illusion of 'righteous access' that sides with those the establishment deems as your child's 'betters' does nothing constructive and only inhibits their rightful access to information. Your teen deserves full access to any and all information that will cultivate the necessary intellectual attributes to future success.

Kids can still be kids while simultaneously learning skills and strategies that can be accessed whenever the interest strikes them. Your child may not understand at this time but their hearts are screaming out for you to guide them and take their corner as they prepare for life. This book series is meant to offer you and your child the information that rightfully belongs to you; unbridled and uncut. With an ever expanding global economy, deflation that defies historical precedence and an education system built out of corruption and illusion, this writer humbly offers you something pure and honest; information that contributes to the preparation of an adult without the educational limitations forced upon them by the establishment.

The topic of 'real' business and proper cybersecurity hygiene have been combined in this three book series because they belong together. Cybersecurity knowledge is a mandatory prerequisite for anyone who works, plays or has connectivity to a virtual environment. Sadly, the traditional school systems, yet again, fail the student and sets them up to be pawns in a cyber-world that will victimize those without the information to protect themselves in cyberspace. Cybersecurity best practices should be second nature for your child as, nowadays, via social media and video games, nearly 50%+ of your teen's life is consumed by online interaction and what steps are being taken to protect them in this space?

One book series can't transform a corrupt education system. One caring parent can't transform an entire student body, but one book and one caring parent can cultivate and guide the mind of one child. This book will guide your child in the topics of: Cybersecurity and best practices, Great Leadership Qualities, How to Write a Press Release, How to Raise Various Types of Investment Capital, How to Avoid Phishing Attacks, How to Defend Against Zero-Day Attacks, and much more.

This book series doesn't have all the answers but this author has concentrated a profound amount of 'rea life' knowledge in this book series based off of the identified shortcomings in his children's public school education. This book series is the result of over three years of research and analyzing curriculum for missing pieces and necessary critical updates to a flawed system. Topics that have been historically categorized for advanced students have been consolidated and presented in an easy to read, fun and informative text for distribution to those seeking a better education for their child.

GREAT LEADERSHIP QUALITIES

Excellent leadership qualities do not come naturally to many, but those who do have them are usually very successful business people. Just because you know how to give instructions, that doesn't make you a good leader. You have to be able to communicate with your staff, keep high morale within your company, commit to your team and business, have a good attitude and mix in some great instinct. Additionally, you should have a good sense of humor to mix into the batch, and you should have plenty of self-assurance. Without the right combination, you may not be able to get through to your staff; and your business will suffer.

BE A GOOD COMMUNICATOR

You may know what you want to tell your staff, but while you are explaining a thought process, some of your employees will look at you with a blank stare. Big Fat Problem. Your business cannot be effective if you cannot communicate your wishes to your staff. Furthermore, poor communication leads to bad morale and high staff turnover – at the least. You could have a low staff turnover, but lose customers because an unhappy staff projects its low morale to customers. Once a customer receives poor treatment or comes to the conclusion that the employees are not happy, that customer may not return.

A customer may not return if he or she thinks you are treating your employees roughly, simply because that customer does not want to support someone who does not respect and trust his or her staff and employees.

If you do get blank stares or notice that employees can't seem to do anything right, the issue may be with your communication skills. To run a successful business, you must be able to succinctly and clearly describe your needs. When you are able to do this, you and your staff will be able to work toward the same goal – you will be able to work as a team.

When your communication skills are top notch, you should be able to easily train your team to be productive and friendly. To help with communication, you should have an open door policy and be available to staff throughout the day. Holding a daily meeting – either in the morning or just before everyone goes home – to discuss any issues also leads to better communication. Your staff needs to know that it can go to you with problems that they cannot handle on their own. The staff also needs to know that you are confident enough to sort the problems out in an effective manner.

Once your staff and employees knows they can trust you to lead them in the right direction and that you are adept at handling whatever comes your way, they will be more apt to work harder and to work as a well-oiled machine.

HAVE A SENSE OF HUMOR

The first thing you think of doing when something goes wrong is to scream and yell. These actions will make your staff very unhappy and they will dread coming to work. If a staff member makes a mistake, surely speak to him or her about it and discuss how to keep that mistake from happening again.

In your discussion, keep your tone even and you can even import your sense of humor once you know the staff member un derstands how to keep from making the same mistake. With excellent communication, you should have hardly any staff errors.

If something happens that is beyond the control of you or your staff member, such as a web site crash or a lost customer due to circumstances beyond your control, treat the situation with a little levity and a sense of humor. Once your staff realizes that you are not going to blow a head gasket every time something goes wrong, they will not be afraid to come to you regarding a potential issue.

If someone comes to you when that person realizes that the company is going to be in the weeds, you might be able to head the problem off before it happens. Excellent communication between you and your staff and between staff members, along with a little humor, can often stop issues before they bury you.

BE SELF-ASSURED

Self-assurance is important when things are not going right– and things will not always be peachy when you own a business. There are times when your brand may come under fire – whether your business is large or small -- because of something a V.I.P. customer says or because of a problem with manufacturing. Stocks may drop and you may see a decline in customers.

It is at this point that you should have a high confidence level and a calm demeanor. When you are calm during a situation, you import that calmness to your staff. This allows them to work confidently and to help restore your brand image. As a business owner or manager, part of your job is to put out the fires that may appear from time to time. If you can fight the fire with confidence and keep your wits about you, your staff will be more responsive, thus extinguishing the flames that much sooner.

MAKING A COMMITMENT

A hard-working team and having quality content means that you work with your team. In addition to management, you also help your staff with their jobs. When your staff and employees see you working hard to make the business work, they also work hard. When you prove your commitment to your brand, your staff and employees will follow suit. When things go wrong – and they will – your staff will back you up and help with damage control. When things are going well, your staff will chip in to make things go even better.

Commitment also means keeping promises. Whether the promise is to your staff, a vendor or a customer, never go back on your word. Keeping promises boosts team morale and shows customers and vendors that they can trust you. It also boosts your reputation as a fair business person.

When you make and keep promises to your staff and employees, they won't make promises to customers and vendors that they can't keep – employees always follow their boss's examples and actions. Your business will become known as an honest business if you keep it honest with your staff and employees.

HAVE AN OPTIMISTIC ATTITUDE

A motivated team is the key to a successful business. Excellent communication skills, working alongside your staff and bonuses keep everyone on an even keel. Depending on the size of your operation, you may provide "extras" for your staff – you may have a water cooler, a well-stocked coffee center, and a small kitchen with a microwave so people can heat up meals, popcorn and hot drinks.

A break room with a kitchen area also gives the staff an informal place to meet for chit-chat or to get advice and help with a project. You might even provide snacks for the employees. You can get things like pretzels and popcorn in bulk. If everyone has the ability to run to the kitchen for a quick snack, their energy levels stay up, and staff morale is high. Remember the old saying "All work and no play..." That applies to you, your staff and your employees. Having a place to take a break from the office makes employees move around and see something other than the four same walls. It may even encourage new ideas – just because of a "change in scenery."

You may even provide beer for those who would like to hang out after work and talk to co-workers about their job or life in general. Providing extras for the staff may seem like small thing, but it shows your employees that you care about them.

You could also set up a bonus system. Whether it is for the person with the highest sales or because someone went over and above in their job duties during the past month, employees always enjoy a surprise bonus. Just be sure to follow through with the bonus system – don't do it for a couple of months, then can the program.

GETTING PEOPLE TO CONTRIBUTE – INCLUDING YOU

If you contribute after hours when you need to, your staff will be more willing to help after hours to keep a customer happy or to finish a report needed the next morning. Furthermore, if the staff and employees see that you put in extra time, they will be more willing to do their best to make sure deadlines are met and customers are happy. When you have a hard-working staff, you have a recipe for success.

It is difficult to ask a staff member or employee to do something that you wouldn't do yourself. If the after-hours job takes two or three people, don't ask the entire staff to stay – ask a couple of people to help you. Remember, the more hands you have and the more brains you have, the faster the work will go – unless you have too many: Then it seems to take three times as long to complete a project because extra people just get in the way.

USE YOUR IMAGINATION

Sometimes you may be forced to veer onto a side road because of unforeseen circumstances. This usually happens when you have a fire to put out or when someone -- usually a customer – doesn't follow the game plan.

When you come up on a problem, use your imagination to come up with a good solution. Involve your staff in deciding the best path to take to get the business – or the customer – back on track. For example, if you are in marketing and you created an over-the-top marketing campaign for a new customer, but the customer hates the idea; you'll have to come up with something else rather quickly or you may lose the account. This is the best time to get all of your staff involved, even those that are not working on that particular campaign. Fresh brains may be able to come up with fresh ideas, and more importantly, the one fresh idea that your customer loves.

Furthermore, it gives you an opportunity to see which employees have additional skills that you may use. You may have just found your next top-notch marketer. Just because someone is in the mail room doesn't mean they don't have excellent ideas. That person may have no self-confidence, but given the chance can really show off. This is an excellent time to boost this employee's morale.

If you are put into a situation where you have to make a choice and both options are bad choices, be sure you think both options through completely – don't make a bad situation worse by making an emotional decision on the fly. Once you've made a decision, ask your staff to punch holes in it – find the bad things about that decision. They may think of something you missed – and the staff will know that you trust them enough to help make a hard decision. If both decisions are not good for the company, but you must make one, choose the decision with the least amount of consequences – as long as it's a moral avenue.

USE YOUR INSTINCT

Eventually, no matter how much experience you have with running a business, you are going to come across a new and different situation. You won't have a roadmap and will have to make decisions on the fly. In addition, the riskier the decision, the more pressure you'll have – not just on you, but on your staff, too.

You can use past experiences that are similar to help you through the decision-making process or you can ask your staff for suggestions. No matter how you make the decision – even with your staff's assistance – you need to guide the staff through the process. Your employees trust you to make the right decision for the company.

Following your instinct and using your natural intuition also helps guide you through a rough time. You can also reach out to your mentors and advisory board for support. Regardless of what anyone suggests, the final decision is up to you – and you will be the one to come to the ultimate decision of what is best for your brand reputation. Once you learn to trust yourself as your employees do, some of these decisions will be easier.

ALWAYS INSPIRE OTHERS

Inspiration is always good, especially if the business is new and off to a slow start. Most businesses do have a rough time the first two or three years and often take a loss. Inspire your team to work through the tough times by ensuring they can see the success that will come because of hard work. Whether you are working with partners or you have a staff that you depend on to get you through the day, all team members must be on board.

You can generate enthusiasm by setting and reviewing smaller, weekly or monthly goals. If you use a three- or five-year goal, it may seem like you aren't getting anything done. However, if you set short-term goals, everyone sees progress and will be more willing to get through the tough times. It's almost like telling yourself, "Ten more yards and I'm halfway through the marathon – I can do it!" Keep a dry-erase board in the kitchen so all employees know where to find the goal status.

If energy levels are falling because of hard work or low morale, give your staff – and yourself – a break. Be sure to tell everyone they are doing a great job and knock off a few hours early or take some time for an office party.

HAVE INTEGRITY

Even if your ethical values are high, you need to hold your business to higher ethical values. Remember, your team and your business are a reflection of you, thus if your business is highly ethical, you are, too. Ethical values tie in with keeping high employee morale and happy customers. Your employees will have the same values as you, so you must "lead the pack" when it comes down to making ethical choices.

BE A CONTRIBUTOR

When you planned your business, you had a vision of what it would take to make it successful. Certain values and core beliefs fit into that success. To ensure a smooth-running operation, you may want to create a list of core beliefs and values; and post them for all employees to see. At the same time, be sure to encourage openness in the office – this is part of your communication skills. If your employees know your values, they will be influenced by those values when they see you sticking to them. They will also be more willing to come to you should they see another employee breaking the standards and core beliefs.

In short, you need to act the same way you expect your employees to act. By contributing to certain core standards and values, your employees will follow suit. Furthermore, you'll find that the workplace will be friendlier as everyone knows what to expect from you and their co-workers. When you have a friendlier workplace, everyone will have higher morale which shows in how the employees work with each other and with customers.

HAVE THE ABILITY TO DELEGATE

One of the most important things you need to be able to do is trust your staff enough to delegate work. If you try to do it all yourself, especially once you pick up more customers, you'll spread yourself too thin and the quality of your work will suffer. You'll also find yourself producing less as you will dread coming in to face the pile of work. Dreading work leads to procrastination.

If you have a large company, you may want to delegate certain tasks to a specific department, but if you are a small company, you can delegate one or more tasks to an individual or a small group of individuals. The ability to delegate tasks is an important skill. It doesn't work if you ask any one person to complete a certain task. You need to be able to choose the right person for a specific task so that the task is done properly and to your specifications.

Delegation doesn't work with just picking a person – be sure the person enjoys the task. You may have three people that have the ability to respond to customer service emails but only one person who enjoys answering emails all day. You'd do better picking the person that enjoys the task, as he or she will look forward to working every day and put more effort into the task.

Choosing staff members or employees to help with specific tasks also shows them that you trust them enough to give them the responsibility. This is great for employee morale. Furthermore, it gives you more time to attend to tasks that absolutely cannot be delegated to employees, such as payroll and other confidential jobs.

SUMMARY

In closing, it might seem like you have to be Superman to be a good leader. After all, this is quite a list. But that is not so – if you stop and take a look at yourself, you may find that you already have many of these qualities.

If you don't have them all, create a list for yourself to refer to when you are not sure of something. Eventually, these leadership qualities will become second hand. If you still have problems creating the perfect office environment and getting people to follow your lead, have a powwow with some of your advisors. They will be able to give you more tips to help you accomplish what you need.

If you treat your employees and staff fairly and let them know you have an open door policy, you will find that the rest of the leadership qualities are easier to achieve.

2

ANYONE CAN BE PWNED THROUGH CHROME EXTENSION HACKS

WHAT IS PWNING THROUGH CHROME EXTENSION HACKS?

Pwning, in hacker jargon, refers to compromising or controlling another's website, computer, application or gateway device. Some security researchers even award Pwnie Awards for cracking.

Although Google claims that its browser, Chrome, is the safest web browser on the market, one can never be too careful in matters concerning security. There are indeed several Chrome extensions with which you could lock down Chrome and make it extremely secure.

However, other extensions of Chrome are not so secure, and can be used by attackers to compromise the Chrome browser. For example, the Scratch-Pad Extension allows users to take notes and auto-syncs the note files with

Google Docs in the ScratchPad folder. One of the features of this extension allows users to share ScratchPad folders without the need for any permission from the original user.

HOW CAN ATTACKERS USE VULNERABLE CHROME EXTENSIONS?

A malicious code hidden in one of the notes saved on the ScratchPad folder, when accessed by the victim can compromise his browser. Once the note is opened, the code proceeds to steal all contacts saved in the victim's Gmail account, since he was already logged into it. Although Google has now patched this specific vulnerability, there are several other extensions with similar or worse vulnerabilities.

With increased use of mobile devices, attacks on applications are rising. Many powerful chrome extensions are meant for the user to access cloud services through Chrome, and this is becoming the main target for attackers.

Most mobile apps require user permission for accessing the various features and capabilities. Extensions for the Chrome OS also require permissions to access features and capabilities, but the difference is, permissions are set and defined by the developer of the extension.

With independent software developers writing the Chrome OS extensions, the security mindset of the developers becomes more important to define the vulnerability/security of the software.

WHAT HAPPENS DURING AN ATTACK ON A VULNERABLE CHROME OS EXTENSION?

With increased focus on cloud-based applications and storage, malware is not downloadable from the cloud to the user's machine. The usual suspects are weeded out by the Chrome OS and users remain protected.

Therefore, instead of targeting the data on the user's hard disk, the attacker targets the applications that send and receive data between the cloud service and the Chrome browser.

Attackers target common web vulnerabilities that can compromise higher privileged applications. They use Cross Site Request Forgery and Cross Site Scripting vulnerabilities, which are the most common in such extensions. As independent developers write most extensions, writing bad code is common, and the developer may provide the extension with more permissions than is necessary.

ONCE EXPLOITED, THE ATTACKER CAN:

- » Monitor all the open tabs on the victim's browser
- » Execute a malicious JavaScript on every tab
- » Extract HTML Code from the web pages
- » Read/Write cookies stored in the browser
- » Access the local hard disk of the victim
- » Manipulate the history of the victim's browser
- » Take screenshots of the tabs on the browser
- » Inject keyloggers/ BeEF hooks for causing further damage

HOW CAN PWNING THROUGH CHROME EXTENSION HACKS BE PREVENTED?

Awareness of which extensions provide greater security to Chrome affords the best protection from these attacks. Some of these extensions enhance the inherent security of the Chrome browser. External vigilance and continuous monitoring for malware, Trojans, and virus is essential. Some of the more secure extensions that help prevent attacks are:

- » Google Alarm
- » FlashBlock
- » BugMeNot Lite
- » AdBlock
- » Secure Profile
- » PasswordFail
- » KB SSL Enforcer
- » View Thru
- » Click & Clean
- » Secbrowsing

- » TrustGuard
- » Credit Card Nanny
- » Web of Trust
- » LastPass
- » SiteAdvisor

REFERENCES:

1. Osborn, K,. Kotowicz, K., *BlackHat USA 2012, Advanced Chrome Extension Exploitation*. Available from: <http://media.blackhat.com/bh-us-12/Briefings/Osborn/BH_US_12_Osborn_Kotowicz_Advanced_Chrome_Extension_Slides.pdf>. [2013].

2. Notebook Review, *15 Best Google Chrome Security Extensions*. Available from: <http://www.notebookreview.com/default.asp?newsID=5796&review=15+Best+Google+Chrome+Security+Extensions>. [10 August 2010].

3. Rashid, F. Y., eWeek, *Google Chrome OS Hacked Using ScratchPad Extension in Black Hat Preview*. Available from:<http://www.eweek.com/c/a/Mobile-and-Wireless/Google-Chrome-OS-Hacked-Using-ScratchPad-Extension-in-Black-Hat-Preview-343583/>. [14 July 2011].

4. Kaplan, D., CRN, *Chrome Extension Hack Pwns Everyone*. Available from: <http://www.crn.com.au/News/266119,chrome-extension-hack-pwns-everyone.aspx>. [8 Aug 2011].

3

HOW TO WRITE A PRESS RELEASE

A press release is one of the best public relations strategies a company can use to get exposure. You can use a press release to announce an event, a product release, new management, a merger or an acquisition among other newsworthy events. This short document should grab a journalist's interest enough to entice him or her to further cover the topic. It's a great way to get free exposure to millions of viewers, readers or listeners, which means thousands – at the very least – of potential customers.

When crafting a press release, you must make it stand out like a sore thumb because journalists see tons of pitches and potential stories every day. The press release format is basic, but the content should be different and riveting, and at the same time, professional. There are eight steps to writing a press release that grabs the reader by the shirt collar and says, "Hey! Pick me!"

CREATE A GREAT HEADLINE

The headline, like the title of a book or great magazine article, is the first thing the reader sees. If the headline doesn't grab the reader's attention, your press release is going to end up in the circular file. The headline is the first thing a reader reads, but it is the last thing that should be written, as you can then choose the most important idea.

Not only should the headline grab the reader's attention, but it should use sales psychology while being very specific. With a specific headline, you are able to communicate the subject of your press release instantly, and show that the content is interesting and new.

Don't use the first headline you come up with – write several, and then pick the best three. You can combine the best parts of each headline and simplify it so that it is short 'n sweet. The headline should make the reader curious, grab his or her emotions and make the reader feast his or her eyes on the rest of the copy.

An excellent headline also uses sales psychology by luring the reader to move past the headline. Don't let the reader give a negative answer to the inherent question contained in the headline. Sales psychology arouses a reader's curiosity and doesn't allow him or her to walk away without reading more.

For example, instead of asking if a person wants Option A or Option B, which could elicit a negative response, ask which option the person wants. While the person could say "neither," the first thing that enters his or her head is, "I need to choose one." Apply this thought process to the headline to encourage the reader to put the press release in the "I need to read this" pile instead of the circular file.

GET TO THE POINT

Don't drag your readers through the entire document without giving them something to latch onto. They'll get bored with it if you don't get to the point right away, then all the work you put into a great headline goes down the drain.

Journalists are busy, so if a headline catches their attention, they will start reading and may only get to the first few sentences, or they may actually read the first sentence and scan the rest of the press release. Thus, you need to get your message to the reader and convince him or her to immediately read further.

If the press release has more than one important point, make sure you reach all of them in the first few sentences.

Additional paragraphs are for supporting information. You might expound on statistics or in the case of an event, discuss the location and happenings at the event. If you are holding a fund raiser and a popular singer is slated to appear, be sure you mention that person or group in the headline, then in later paragraphs for additional information.

INCLUDE STATISTICS AND HARD NUMBERS

When you support the significance of your announcement with hard numbers, you create compelling content. This is especially important if you're claiming a trend such as the popularity of a certain designer or a statistic for a city.

For example, if a criminal defense attorney states that his city has one of the highest murder rates, he or she may find the murder rate plus other rate breakdowns such as murder in the commission of burglary or murder during a domestic violence dispute for his or her city. Often, governmental web sites – federal, state and local – may have this information. Colleges and other groups that conduct studies may have statistics listed on their web sites.

An example for a fundraiser event with a popular singer would be to introduce a popular singer and mention that the person won awards or sells out every concert. Provide the number of awards and attendance numbers, e.g., five Grammys and sellout crowds averaging 60,000 people.

PERFECTION RULES

Proofreading is an important part of creating the perfect press release. Once you write it, proofread it carefully. Let it go until the next morning then proofread it again. Because it is very difficult to catch your own mistakes, have two or three friends or co-workers proofread the press release. Be sure to tell them to be harsh in their criticism as some friends might tell you that it looks great instead of being honest.

Just one mistake can make a reader discard your press release as he or she will not take you seriously. Press releases must be professional, which means perfect spelling and grammar.

Another tip for proofreading is to convert the text to another format. You can convert a Word document to Adobe or you can increase the font in the Word document. Doing this often makes mistakes stand out because of the different format or text size.

INCLUDING QUOTATIONS

A quote from someone in the company or from someone involved with manufacturing the product or setting up the event can add flavor to the press release. A quote also provides additional information about the product, service or event.

You can ask an employee for a quote, or you may remember something catchy that someone said while discussing the topic contained in the press release. Be sure you ask the employee if you can use his or her name and the quote. If the press release does get published, that person's name and quote will be in front of a lot of people.

The quote could be something humorous or it could be a statistic from the manufacturer of a product. Regardless of what you choose, make sure it makes the product, service or event stand out.

CONTACT INFORMATION

Don't forget to include your contact information in the press release. Without it, the press release is ineffective. If a journalist cannot get in touch with you to get more information, he or she will not publish an otherwise great press release. You should put your contact information at the top of the press release, and it should include, at a minimum, your phone number and email address.

Your contact information also allows a journalist to call you back at a later time to ask if you'd like to do a follow up article on the event. A follow up interview may include how much you money you collected in a fundraiser, how you changed a person's life because of certain services or even a donation of your retail sales to help someone down on his or her luck. This is more free advertising for your company or group.

If your press release is about your company going public you could create a follow up press release to tell people how well your stock sold on its first day; and if you are selling private stock, what your expansion plans are for the next year.

KEEP IT SHORT 'N SWEET

Limit the press release to one page if possible. If you have to use a second page, it is acceptable, but keep in mind that the shorter the press release, the better. This forces you to delete any information that is not important or that doesn't convey urgency. Because a journalist is usually limited on space, he or she looks for stories that are short and to the point.

To get the best information in the press release, write without any constrictions. Read through the document and delete any information that doesn't convey urgency and importance to the reader. This information can be presented on the web site or in additional documentation through email. When you are done, you should have a document that tells the reader the most important information about the event.

PROVIDING ACCESS TO MORE INFORMATION

Though you should limit your press release to one or two pages, that doesn't mean you can't give people more information. Include links to your web site in the press release. Make sure the web site has more information that directly relates to the content in the press release. If the content is on a separate page on your web site, provide the direct link instead of making the reader go to the main page to search for the content.

You might include your mission, a few paragraphs about what you've previously accomplished and more information about the product, service or event.

If you do not have a web site, offer an email with additional information. Ask readers to send an email to you for more information. You can set up an auto-responder to send a document containing more information about the event or product.

If you are doing a follow up press release, create a new web page with the event statistics. If your press release was about raising money by selling stock, keep people apprised of your expansion progress. These are things to keep people coming back to your web site, thus in the front of their minds.

EXAMPLES OF GREAT HEADLINES

A criminal defense attorney may use "New Report Identifies Cities with Highest Murder Rate" to let the world know he or she defends those accused of manslaughter or murder if his city is listed in the report.

A museum might use "Lost Works of [famous artist] Found in [city] Attic" to let people know it has a new exhibit with these works of art.

A retailer might announce beating a goal by using a headline that states, "[Retailer] Beats Goal of 10,000 Sales for Third Quarter." This headline will get people to read it simply because they want to know how many sales the retailer actually had. An entity holding a fundraiser may use a celebrity's name in the headline: "Wildlife Sanctuary Fundraiser Features [celebrity name]." In this case, if the press release is also published online, it will garner the attention of those searching that celebrity's name. People who would not have searched for your fundraiser would see it.

SUMMARY

Creating a great press release is not something you can do in a matter of minutes. It takes a great deal of thought and planning. To get to the meat of the whole document, start with rambling thoughts about the product or event. Write everything down, whether you do it in paragraph form or in list form. If you do work better with the paragraph form, be sure to keep each thought in its own paragraph.

Get other pertinent information you would like to see in the press release, including statistics and quotations. Once you have everything you need, find the most important aspects of what you need to convey. These should make up your first paragraph. One of the statistics should be in the first paragraph.

Everything else is considered additional information and needs to go into subsequent well-organized paragraphs.

Once you have completed the entire press release, create an attention-grabbing title that will keep the press release in front of the reader's eyeballs long enough to keep his or her interest. If it keeps the reader's interest, there is a good chance the journalist will choose your press release for publishing.

4

CRIME OVERCOMES ENCRYPTED SESSIONS OF MAJOR BROWSERS

Meta Description: *Major browsers use sessions that, although encrypted, allow attackers to decrypt the user's sessions*

WHAT IS CRIME?

Servers use HTTP Secure or HTTPS traffic to encrypt user authentication cookies. For this, they use the Transport Layer Security or TLS, Secure Socket Layer or SSL, and a protocol named SPDY (pronounced Speedy), which decrypts the cookies that the user sends for authentication. The CRIME attack exploits the data compression scheme to collect information about the user.

HOW IS A CRIME ATTACK DONE?

CRIME uses brute force to remember authenticated users by decrypting the HTTPS cookies that the website sets. Usually, a website returns cookies that authenticate the user when the user sends their credentials to the website. The CRIME attack code, planted as a malware in the user's computer, forces the browser used by the victim to send specially modified HTTPS requests to the targeted website. Once the request is compressed and returned by the server, CRIME analyzes them to determine the value of the cookie for the session.

WHAT HAPPENS DURING A CRIME ATTACK?

Once the cookie is decoded, the attacker can return to the site visited by the user and login using the collected credentials. The attacker masquerading as the authentic user may steal important information. Without the knowledge of the user, fraudulent financial transactions may steal money from bank accounts.

Attackers plant a JavaScript code in the user's computer. This code runs when the user works with his browser. The code sniffs or analyzes the victim's HTTPS traffic, and decrypts session cookies. The attack succeeds only if both the client and the server support the data compression-decompression feature used by the SSL/TLS/SPDY.

Almost all servers use SSL and TLS for rendering their HTTPS traffic, however, Google and Firefox use SPDY, also a networking protocol with compression, multiplexing and prioritization for reducing the time that web pages take to load. SPDY does not actually replace either HTTP or HTTPS, but it helps to speed up data transfer.

The culprit is the compression technique or algorithm that SSL, TLS and SPDY use. This algorithm, DEFLATE, eliminates duplicate strings. The algorithm replaces repeated strings with a small token on each request and the length of the request will reduce with each repeat request.

CRIME analyzes the difference in consecutive requests to guess the value of the cookie. By repeatedly sending requests to the server, it tries to re-generate the information that is being encrypted. Although it is not possible to directly read the session cookie that is included in the requests as the browser uses many security mechanisms, CRIME controls the path of each new request by inserting different strings into the request and attempting to match the 5 value of the cookie.

Even though session cookies can be long and may contain digits, lower-case letters and uppercase letters, special algorithms in CRIME help to avoid making a large number of requests for decrypting them. Sometimes CRIME requires only four requests and at the most six may be needed.

HOW TO PREVENT SUCCESSFUL CRIME

CRIME needs to plant the JavaScript code into the victim's computer for the attack to be fruitful. Therefore, the user has to protect his system and network from an outside attack and also an inside attack. Anti-malware, anti-spyware and anti-virus software programs must be used and the network hardened with proper security systems such as firewalls and security policies.

For CRIME to succeed, both the server and the client should be using the same compression/decompression techniques/protocols. Using the latest versions of browsers mitigates the problem, as many have patched up their code and are no longer using the compression algorithms. Google has modified SPDY to avoid attacks from CRIME.

REFERENCES:

1. Fisher, D., Threat Post, *New Attack Uses SSL/TLS Information Leak to Hijack HTTPS Sessions*. Available from: <http://threatpost.com/new-attack-uses-ssltls-information-leak-hijack-https-sessions-090512/>. [5 September2012].

2. Constantin, L., ComputerWorld, *'CRIME' attack abuses SSL/TLS data compression feature to hijack HTTPS sessions.* Available from: <http://news.idg.no/cw/art.cfm?id=976ED08F-CB4A-23DA-FFD-A0419B8750B72>.[14 September 2012].

3. Goodin, D., ARS Technica, *Crack in Internet's foundation of trust allows HTTPS session hijacking.* Available from: <http://arstechnica.com/security/2012/09/crime-hijacks-https-sessions/>. [13 September 2011].

5

DIFFERENT KINDS OF CAPITAL

Depending on how a business is set up, it could have up to five types of capital. Capital is the money you put into the business. In general, capital is assets that the business owns such as cash, machinery, real estate, accounts receivable and inventory. It takes money to buy all of these things to get a business started – that money has to come from somewhere, whether you put it in yourself, you borrow it or you get vendors to stock your shelves and allow you to pay for items as you sell them.

Don't think of capital as just cash – it is the amount of financial resources the owner has to execute his or her business plan. You need capital to develop a product, for sales and marketing, the legal formation of the company, administrative support, and to purchase real estate and inventory.

EQUITY CAPITAL – OWNER OR VENTURE CAPITALIST FUNDED

Equity capital is the most understood form of capital. It is the net worth of the business and is figured by subtracting the liabilities from the assets. It is also more favored than any other type of capital since it is difficult to go into bankruptcy. Some sources say it is impossible to go bankrupt, but if the business falters and you must sell the equipment to pay the bills, you won't be able to continue manufacturing. You'll avoid bankruptcy, but you won't have the equipment to continue operating.

If you have a business that does not require a lot of capital to start, it is very difficult to go bankrupt in the event of a major financial catastrophe such as a major recession. For example, a sole proprietor attorney may invest $20,000 to start up, which includes renting his or her office, purchasing computers and office supplies, utilities and hiring a paralegal. If the business slows, he can simply lay off the paralegal and do the work himself. The chance of losing everything – unless he has no new clientele – is slim to none.

When you use equity capital, it takes a lot of work to grow a business, but if you can generate returns that are high enough, your business can have a pure equity capital structure instead of a combination of this and other types of capital.

When a business is funded with only equity capital, the owners and/or shareholders put in all of the cash and there are no liabilities offsetting the assets. The owners do not usually set terms for the company to pay back the equity, but instead, have a right to the future earnings. Owners may be paid with distributions or dividends as long as the company is profitable and has enough cash flow. Yes, the owners are paid last.

If the owners do not have the cash to support the execution of their business plan, they can enter into an agreement with a venture capitalist, who invests the capital under certain terms and conditions. The venture capitalist agrees to a percentage of future earnings, conversion rights or to hold a spot on the board of directors instead of repayment.

A venture capitalist does not receive payments on his or her investments, thus you will most likely have to provide a business plan that outlines your future financial picture. The investor will complete due diligence before making the investment, and that includes determining whether the business will survive long enough to make the investment worthwhile. The only way a venture is worthwhile to a venture capitalist is if it will pay more over time than the investor would have received if had loaned the money to the business owner.

Your business plan should show what other money you will be investing in the venture, how much profit you plan for each sale, how many sales you anticipate per day, month, quarter or year, and how you plan on attracting more customers over time.

DEBT CAPITAL – INTEREST ONLY LOANS

Debt capital is also a popular way to fund businesses, simply because it is relatively easy to get. A business borrows money from a bank, a wealthy person, or bondholders and pays interest on the money. The business does not pay anything on the principal. The parties sign a contract stating that the business will pay the principal back on a certain date. The borrowed money is the capital and the interest is the cost of debt. You may have heard such loans being referred to as interest only loans.

Profits are realized after taxes and interest payments. For example, if you borrow $100,000 at 10 percent interest and earn 15 percent after taxes, you have a 5 percent profit.

Furthermore, the interest payments are tax deductible while the dividends paid on equity capital are not. Debt capital also allows a company to continue making a profit indefinitely as long as the company makes a high enough return to cover the interest payments.

The disadvantage of using debt capital is that the interest payments must be paid on time. With equity capital, if the money is not there, the owners do not get paid, and there are no consequences. Should the company lose sales, whether because of the economy or any other reason, it has to find the money to pay the interest payments or the lender can recall the loan.

Before a company decides to use debt equity, it must take a hard look at the economy and other factors that will financially affect the company. The best way to do this is to create a business plan. Furthermore, most investors will require the owner to submit a business plan as part of the investor's due diligence. It is very difficult to get debt capital without a business plan that outlines the business's anticipated growth over a five-year period.

As with obtaining equity capital through a venture capitalist, you must show anticipated profits and traffic flow. If the investor does not think your business plan is solid enough to show enough profit to pay the loan, the investor will deny funding.

SPECIALTY CAPITAL

Some forms of capital – negative cash conversion and float capital – have very little economic cost associated with it. These forms of capital allow your company to grow unheeded. Sweat equity is another form that has very little economic cost associated with it, but if you consider that time is money, it does have more cost than negative cash conversion and float capital. Your only limitation is how many hours per day you are willing to put into your business. Businesses generally grow faster if you can secure – or at least partially secure – at least one type of special capital.

NEGATIVE CASH CONVERSION OR VENDOR FINANCING

» Negative cash conversion is also known as vendor financing. If you can get vendors to front you inventory, your initial capital investment will be significantly lower. The best way to understand negative cash conversion is to compare it with consignments.

» The vendor stocks your store with its products. You do not pay the vendor until you sell the product. As soon as you sell an item, the vendor sells it to you. You must then pay the vendor for the item you sold. Your contract with the vendor may be on a weekly or monthly basis. The vendor may also require you to pay for the sold items after you sell a certain number.

» If you can get a vendor to stock your store without upfront payment, you can carry much more inventory; and this allows you to build your business much quicker. You won't have to worry about ordering an item that is too expensive to keep in inventory. Furthermore, negative cash conversion allows you to expand your business – to a larger store or to multiple locations – much quicker than if you had to buy more inventory.

» Negative cash conversion also allows you to generate more income than other types of capital. You can measure vendor financing by comparing the percentage of inventory to the percentage of accounts payable and by reviewing the cash conversion cycle. When comparing percentages, the higher the percentage, the better. When you analyze the cash conversion, more negative days are better than positive days.

» If you plan to use negative cash conversion as a form of equity, be sure to outline this in the business plan. Furthermore, you must show the investor how you are going to obtain enough sales and retain customers to make it worthwhile to stock your store with inventory. Many vendors will not allow you to stock without payment unless you can show that you will sell a certain number of units in a set amount of time.

FLOATING CAPITAL – IT'S NOT YOUR MONEY

» You've heard the sayings that "time is money" and "don't use your own money to start a business." Floating capital combines those two sayings for one of the best forms of capital – if you can make it work.

» Floating capital is income that is generated and invested before you have to pay it out. The best example of a floating capital business is an insurance company. The insurance company collects money from people for insurance policy premiums, and then invests the money. It can do this because it does not need to pay out the money right away.

» A person may pay his or her insurance premiums for several years before the insurance company needs to pay out on a claim filed by that person. Basically, floating capital is money held by a company, but not owned by the company. In some cases, the cost of capital is negative. In other words, the small cost of floating capital is offset by income from investments.

» While this type of capital works great for insurance companies, it is very difficult for other types of companies to develop floating capital. Floating capital can also bite you in the butt. For example, if you provide home insurance and a hurricane wipes out most of your customer's homes, you'll have to pay out on every one of those policies. If you don't have enough return on your investments or you can't liquidate the investments, you won't have enough to pay the claims.

» Your business plan should outline contingencies should Mother Nature – or another destructive force -- decide to wreak havoc on your financial stability.

SWEAT EQUITY

» Sweat equity is not really a form of capital in the sense that there is no upfront cash, and most of it is intangible. However, time is money, thus the owner's time can be considered as capital. Generally, the owner puts in long hours at little to no pay. Since he or she doesn't have to pay someone else to do the work, the owner saves quite a bit of payroll expense and tax.

» Sweat equity can work in many different situations. In the initial building phase, if the owner does some of the construction himself, he or she can get a discount on a general contractor's fees, since that is one less person the general contractor needs to pay. If the business is up and running and the owner works in the store, that is one less person he or she has to pay.

» You often hear the term "sweat equity" associated with building a personal home, but it can be used in any situation where the owner can put in the hours instead of paying someone else to do the work.

» For example, if a retail salesperson gets paid $10 per hour and works 40 hours, the owner saves $400 per week. Additionally, the owner would have to pay payroll taxes for the employee, worker's compensation insurance and other costs associated with payroll. These costs could easily add up to a couple hundred per week, especially if the owner provides health insurance for the employees.

» Before you enter into a sweat equity agreement, be sure you understand the terms. Also, be sure that the contractor properly discounts his services. You are not gaining anything if the contractor would normally pay a carpenter $50,000 per job but only discounts his fee by $10,000 in exchange for your hard labor.

SUMMARY

The type of capital you use depends on your current financial position and the type of business you are starting. If you created a new invention and planned to manufacture it yourself, you will need a ton of capital to purchase the manufacturing plant, the equipment and machines, and all of the "small things" such as office furniture and supplies. In a case such as this, you may use a combination of equity capital, debt capital, sweat equity.

If you are opening a retail store you might use equity and debt capital, plus add some sweat equity and negative cash conversion.

When you draft your business plan, you need to keep the types of equity in mind so you can determine whether you need to borrow. If you need to borrow (debt capital), you will need to show the investor – via the business plan – what you expect out of the business for at least five years.

The investor will want to see demographics, how many sales you plan to make per month and how you intend to get the sales. He or she will also need to see your profits. For example, if you are selling an item, how many do you have to sell so that the profit covers the payment to the investor and the operating expenses such as payroll, utilities and the mortgage or rent.

You'll find advantages and disadvantages to all types of capital. When deciding your business structure and financial plans, you may consider all types of capital, but be sure to use the type that best benefits your business. You could even use a combination of several types of capital to best benefit your financial picture.

6

HOW TO AVOID PHISHING ATTACKS FROM TRUSTED THIRD PARTIES

WHAT IS PHISHING FROM TRUSTED THIRD PARTIES?

You may receive a message, purportedly sent by the National Credit Union Administration, with a request to click the provided link for updating your data. To enter the site, you have to enter your credentials, and this is the exact information the phisher wanted.

If the phishers have access to your bank account, they may withdraw money from your bank. However, this will leave an electronic trail, which is not very easy to get rid of and the law enforcement authorities will be in hot pursuit. Therefore, instead of cleaning out your bank account, the phishers prefer to sell your credentials to other fraudsters who operate with more sophistication and who can erase their trail when emptying your bank account.

Trusted third parties such as banks, e-auction and e-pay systems are the major targets that phishers use. They make a fake site that closely resembles the original. The user will generally not suspect anything amiss and they enter their username and password thinking they are accessing the original site.

In a similar way, phishers also target the use's email credentials, which they sell to other fraudsters who distribute viruses or create zombie networks.

DIFFERENT TRICKS THAT PHISHERS USE

Phishers use links, which they design to look very similar to the URLs of credible sites. Less experienced users are easily fooled by these links. More experienced users will be able to notice the difference and avoid clicking on them. Such fake links often begin with an IP address, which credible sites do not commonly use.

A phishing message may look like or imitate an eBay notification. Although the body of the message may contain a link to take the user to the legitimate site, the URL itself may be different. There may be other links to the official site, but the link that requires the user to enter their credentials will lead to the fake site.

A new trend has started on the Internet called 'Pharming'. Pharmers also target access credentials, and they obtain their data via official websites, unlike phishers who send emails to entice their victims.

Phishers mostly target financial sites such as PayPal, eBay and most of the banks. Although most phishing attacks are random, they can be targeted as well. For targeted attacks, fraudsters make certain that a user has an account in a certain bank, before they launch a targeted attack to gain his credentials for the bank site. Although the targeted method means more complications and greater expense for the phishers, the payoff is also higher, as there is a greater chance that the victim will be hooked.

Apart from identity theft, a phishing link may present a far more sinister threat. Phishers may be able to plant spyware, malware, a Trojan program or a key logger in the user's system, once they have the username and password of the victim. Therefore, even if the user does not have a bank account the phisher may steal, the user may not be entirely safe.

HOW TO PROTECT YOURSELF FROM PHISHING:

Scams

It is better to err on the side of caution. Unless you are absolutely confident of the genuineness of the email, it would be prudent to dismiss it as a fraud. Sending username, passwords, account numbers and any other confidential or personal information via email should be avoided at all times. Delete the email immediately (in case the phisher has also sent a malware along) and call the customer service of the sender of the email to verify the legitimacy.

You must use only the latest generation of web browsers. The latest IE and Firefox have built in protection against phishing, and your browser should be able to warn you against phishing and pharming attacks.

REFERENCES:

1. Tschabitscher, H., About.com Guide, *Phishing*. Available from: <http://email.about.com/od/staysecureandprivate/g/phishing.htm>. [?].

2. Kaspersky Lab, *What is phishing?* Available from: <http://www.securelist.com/en/threats/spam?chapter=85>.[2013].

3. Bradley, T., *Internet/Network Security, Protect Yourself From Phishing Scams*. Available from: <http://netsecurity.about.com/od/security101/a/phishprotect.htm>.[?].

7

WHAT IS A DIRECT PUBLIC OFFERING?

Direct public offering implies that the company raises capital by issuing it shares directly to its own suppliers, distributors, employees, customers and friends in the community. These are an alternative to broker-dealer firms.

Direct public offerings are significantly less costly than traditional underwritten offerings. DPOs also don't carry restrictions that are usually stringed to the bank and venture capital financing.

PREREQUISITES OF FILING

» Preparation of the Prospectus. The official offering document is known as Prospectus and is incorporated in the registration statement filed with the SEC. It is inclusive of all details related to company.

» Reporting and Disclosure. All the reporting and disclosure requirements should align with the offering else it would be considered as the violation of state or Federal law.

» States' Regulatory Issues. The DPO must be registered in every state where the company wishes to sell stock. While most of the states accept a form U-7 for the filing, yet many states have different and/or additional regulations and filing fee structures.

» Subscription Agent. The agent is required to ensure the company's compliance with varying state restrictions. Care should be taken to avoid penalties.

» Accounting. An audited financial statement may be required depending on the nature of the offering. Any licensed CPA can provide such services.

» Attorney. To complete the offering in full compliance, an attorney will be needed.

» Financial Printing. There are certain documents, like the printing, inventory and delivery of stock certificates; safeguarding unissued certificates, etc, required for the offering.

FUND OBTAINED FROM DPO

From the theoretical perspective, a company can raise a large amount of money from direct public offering, but that is not the case in practical due to organizational limitations involved in achieving that level of stock sales.

Currently, the maximum limits, which can be raised using various forms of the Direct Public Offering, are:

» SCOR (Reg D) -- $1 Million

» Regulation A -- $5 Million

» SB1 -- $10 Million

» SB2 -- $25 Million

BENEFITS OF DPO

The expense part for direct public offering, when compared to initial public offering is less. There are no underwriters in direct public offerings because they are issued through officers and directors. Unlike an IPO, the shares in DPO are directly marketed to parties that may be interested in the company stocks, and the buyers generally include customer, distributor, or employees.

There are companies which are not very large and cannot get the benefit from the initial public offering. Direct public offering is an attractive alternative to them. Many consider the biggest advantage of a direct public offering is the fact that capital raised doesn't have to be paid back. Corporations can give up a share of the company for the funds it requires. Often, those funds are obtained with far less intensity than what could have been expected with a venture capital firm.

Often the company finds it more suitable to raise funds through a direct public offering than through a traditional debt financing like a bank loan. This turns out to be true where the business involves high risk that involves little physical capital that could be used as security. A direct public offering enables the corporation to market it to those who are more capable of understanding and bearing the risk.

DRAWBACKS

Although Direct Public offering enjoys various benefits it has few drawbacks. The process is not straightforward, and an immense deal of information is to be collected to prepare a registration statement to file with the SEC. Similar to an initial public offering, a direct public offering can deflect the concentration of employees for many months. The difference between the costs of DPO and IPO is not very much. In DPO though the money is not spent on underwriters but a part of that will be invested in marketing efforts.

FEDERAL GOVERNMENT CONSIDERATION

The Security and Exchange commission is the historical federal regulator of Public offering activities, and it allows individual states to regulate securities offerings under $1 million. The last major problem linked with being public a company was the reporting requirements. In 1992, the SEC's Small Business Initiatives simplified the reporting rules and minimized the costs of compliance with federal securities laws.

8

HOW TO BLOCK ZERO-DAY APPLICATION EXPLOITS

WHAT IS A ZERO-DAY APPLICATION EXPLOIT?

Cyber criminals develop newer methods of bypassing security controls when installing malware on corporate endpoints. For example, the newly discovered APT or Advanced Persistent Threat malware uses multiple evasion techniques for bypassing many of the latest detection approaches being utilized. The malware executes only when there is some mouse activity. This action helps it to avoid being detected in the first stage.

In a zero-day exploit, the malware takes advantage of security vulnerability before the weakness becomes known, or on the same day that the vulnerability is discovered. There can be many zero days between initial discovery of the vulnerability and the first attack, before the vulnerability is patched.

WHAT HAPPENS IN A ZERO-DAY APPLICATION EXPLOIT?

In general, the discovery of a potential security issue in a software program leads to a notification to the software company, and in most cases, to the world at large. The software company takes some time to fix its code, before it is ready to distribute a software update or a patch. Even if a potential attacker becomes aware of the vulnerability, it would take him some time to exploit the issue. Meanwhile, hopefully, the software company will make the fix available first.

However, sometimes the attacker is the first to discover the vulnerability. Since no one else knows about the vulnerability, there is obviously no guard against it being exploited.

Blacklisting usually fails in such cases, because cyber criminals keep changing their tactics to avoid detection. Enterprises trying to use application control or whitelisting find to their dismay that it is nearly impossible to control, as the whitelist becomes very large. The number of files they need to review and validate is extraordinarily large, significantly delaying the deployment.

HOW CAN ZERO-DAY APPLICATION EXPLOITS BE KEPT UNDER CONTROL?

The following methods are recommended to prevent enterprises from being exposed to zero-day application exploits:

» Using IPsec or virtual LANs for protecting contents of individual transmissions;

» Deploying an intrusion detection system;

» Introducing network access control for preventing malicious machines from gaining access to the network;

» Locking down the wireless access points and using a security scheme such as WPA2 or Wi-Fi Protected Access for providing maximum protection against wireless-based attacks.

An endpoint malware protection paradigm helps by controlling malware from reaching the endpoint device and installing itself. Even if the malware is able to bypass the security successfully, the enterprise must have detection programs in place to prevent it from functioning.

Advanced data-stealing malware can be stopped from reaching the endpoint devices by new approaches such as the Stateful Application Control. This has two components: the first prevents malware from installing itself on the device; the second prevents malware from executing on the device. The application exploit prevention, as the first layer is called, is an application of whitelisting to the application states, rather than to the applications themselves.

REFERENCES:

1. Rouse, M., *Search Security, zero-day exploit.* Available from: <http://searchsecurity.techtarget.com/definition/ zero-day-exploit>. [July 2010].

2. Tamir, D., *Business security, Can we end zero-day exploits?* Available from: <http://biztechreport.co.uk/2013/04/ can-we-end-zero-day-exploits/>. [14 April 2013].

3. Tubin, G., *Help Net Security, Blocking zero-day application exploits: A new approach for APT prevention.* Available from: <http://www.net-security.org/article.php?id=1824>. [3 April 2013].

9

SEC RULES FOR CYBER SECURITY DISCLOSURE

In May 2011, Senator Jay Rockefeller requested to the Securities and Exchange Commission that it should advice public companies on the time when disclosure of cyber security risk to investors is compulsory. On October 13th, the Division of Corporate Finance at the SEC issued a Disclosure Guidance that for the first time advises registrants to evaluate their cyber security risks and if found necessary these risks should be disclosed to investors. The companies which ignore the suggestion of Division of corporate finance and fail to disclose important cyber security risks do so at their own risk and are liable to regulatory and legal action.

Irrespective of their area of business, be it banking retail or defense industry, companies are facing diverse array of cyber security risks, on a daily basis, from the cyber criminals who attempt on stealing the important and vulnerable information or corrupt data.

OVERVIEW OF THE DISCLOSURE GUIDANCE

The SEC staff states that its Disclosure Guidance is "consistent with the relevant disclosure considerations that arise in connection with any business risk." The disclosure regulations say that SEC is aware of the fact that detailed cyber disclosure could compromise cyber security issues. In this regard, the SEC rules do not require disclosure that would compromise a company's cyber security. Instead, it states that companies should "provide sufficient disclosure to allow investors to appreciate the nature of the risks faced by the particular registrant in a manner that would not have that consequence."

The Disclosure Guidance concedes that existing SEC disclosure rules do not openly refer cyber security matters but states that such revelations may still be mandatory under existing SEC rules. Important information in connection with cyber security risks and cyber incidents are required to be disclosed as and when necessary, to ensure other required disclosures are not misleading in light of the circumstances under which they are made.

The cyber security disclosure is similar to SEC 2010 interpretative release in accordance with SEC climate change disclosure. The Disclosure Guidance makes available the SEC staff's thoughts on the application of existing SEC disclosure rules to cyber security matters. Particularly, the Disclosure Guidance addresses disclosure contemplations appropriate to both cyber security risks and cyber incidents under the following provisions:-

RISK FACTORS

Risk factor disclosed under Item 503 should comprise a discussion of cyber security and cyber incidents if such issues are one of the most important factors that make an investment in the company perilous or tentative. The risk factor disclosures of cyber security should be made according to the individual company's facts and circumstances and should keep away from "boilerplate" disclosures.

Management's Discussion and Analysis (MD&A) of Financial Condition and Results of Operations

Under Item 303, the MD&A should comprise a discussion of cyber security risks and occurrence if cyber incidents are probably capable of leaving an impact on company's liquidity, results of operations or financial condition or would cause reported financial information not to be essentially investigative of future operating result or financial condition.

DESCRIPTION OF BUSINESS

The cyber incidents should be discussed by the public companies in their Business description if these incidents significantly impact a company's products and services, relationships with customers or suppliers, or competitive conditions. The disclosure should encompass the impact of the cyber incidents on each reportable segment.

LEGAL PROCEEDINGS

If there is any pending legal proceeding involving a cyber-incident in which the company or any of its subsidiary is a party to the litigation, companies need to disclose about that legal proceeding.

FINANCIAL STATEMENT DISCLOSURES

Cyber security risks and cyber incidents may have major effects on a company's financial statements. Companies should make sure that any such impact to financial statements is accounted for pursuant to applicable accounting guidance.

DISCLOSURE CONTROLS AND PROCEDURES

It may be possible that a cyber-event might disturb the company's capacity to provide the SEC with the information necessary to be disclosed on SEC filings; in such case the company may conclude that its disclosure controls and procedures are futile.

10

THE COLLATERAL DAMAGE OF PHPSESSID ATTACKS

WHAT IS A BRUTEFORCE OF PHPSESSID ATTACK?

Many websites offer to keep you logged in ("remember me on this website") after you have logged in. This may be convenient in that you do not have to log in repeatedly if you are visiting the site frequently. However, for an attacker on the prowl, you become an easy target as an attacker can go into the website masquerading as you. In technical jargon, the way the attacker learns both your username and passwords and can then impersonate you is Bruteforce of PHPSESSID or session fixation.

WHAT HAPPENS DURING THE ATTACK?

During session fixation, an attacker snooping around can get a valid session ID from an application. The attacker then forces the application to use the same session ID. He does this by sending the victim a link to a website with the session ID attached to the URL. Once the victim uses the link, the attacker uses the information to guess the username and password of the user, and the website the user was visiting. It is then easy for the attacker to impersonate the user.

On the server side, the PHP framework issues a session token when a client session is started. The token comprises a lot of information such as the IP address of the client, current time in seconds and microseconds, a combined PHP lcg sample and optionally additional information (entropy) from available sources.

Even though the PHP string is a big string and MD5 encrypted, the session ID string follows a definite pattern, with parameters such as the IP address and the PHP_combined_lcq at specific places. To generate the actual values by guessing them would take a lot of effort by ordinary means and this is where the brute force technology comes in. The attacker systematically tries every possible combination of symbols, letters and numbers until he discovers the one correct combination that works.

However, depending on the length of the password used, the number of permutations and combinations could be extremely huge to be of practical use and it may take the attacker years to find one password. Attackers therefore use dictionary words, wordlists and smart rulesets to start with, and this could put all accounts at risk by flooding your site with unnecessary traffic.

WHAT IS THE HARM CAUSED BY SUCH ATTACKS?

An attacker trying to guess username and passwords may send a huge number of requests to the server, flooding the server with traffic and causing a denial of service to the authentic users.

Once he gains entry into a vulnerable user account, not only can the attacker steal sensitive information from the account, he can also plant malware that may compromise other accounts as well.

Using the compromised server, the attacker can turn it into a zombie and attach it to his botnet to create further attacks that are more powerful.

HOW CAN SUCH ATTACKS BE PREVENTED?

Usually some very effective mechanisms are used to prevent such attacks. One is to login the user only from a certain IP address. If there is a change in the IP address during a login session, another level of authentication of secret questions is used to identify if the user is genuine. Therefore, even if the attacker has managed to guess the username and password by the brute force method, there is another deterrent to gain access.

Other effective methods used are:

- » Assigning unique login URLs to a section of the users in blocks

- » Preventing automatic attacks by using CAPTCHA

- » Place the attacked account in a lockdown mode with limited capabilities

- » Combinations of the above.

REFERENCES:

1. Susser, B., *Not So Random Numbers. Take Two- The Bruteforce pf PHPSESSID.* Avaliable from: <http://bot24.blogspot.in/2012/09/not-so-random-numbers-taketwo.html>. [6 September 2012].

2. ZZO *The Researcher, PHPSESSID information leakage.* Avaliable from: <http://dev-zzo.net/blog/2013/04/phpsessid-information-leakage/>. [6 April 2013].

3. Burnett, M., *System Administration Database, Blocking Brute Force Attacks.* Avaliable from: <http://www.cs.virginia.edu/~csadmin/gen_support/brute_force.php>. [2007].

11

CONTROLLING ADMINISTRATIVE PRIVILEGES

WHAT HAPPENS IF ADMINISTRATIVE PRIVILEGES ARE NOT UNDER CONTROL?

One of the primary ways for an attacker to gain entry into an enterprise network is by misusing the administrative privileges. Attackers usually follow one of two methods for gaining access. In the first method, the attacker manages to fool one of the privileged users of a workstation into opening a document from a malicious website, or surf a website hosting malicious content, which automatically exploits the visitor's browser.

The malicious code then runs on the victim's computer, and if the victim user's account has administrative privileges, takes over their computer completely. After this it is relatively simple for the attacker to install sniffers, keystroke loggers, and various remote control software to then dig out administrative passwords thus gaining access to sensitive data. Such attacks are common through e-mails. If an unsuspecting administrator were to open an e-mail containing an infected attachment, the attacker gains access to the system using this as a pivot point to attack other systems.

Attackers may also gain access by a secondary method: guessing or cracking a password used by an administrator. This gives the attacker access to the target machine.

With administrative privileges distributed widely and loosely, the attacker's work of compromising these privileges is made easier since so many other accounts are now available.

HOW DOES THIS AFFECT THE ENTERPRISE?

An administrator has absolute privileges over the entire enterprise network. If the attacker were able to elevate his privileges equal to the level of an administrator, then he could masquerade as the administrator himself and quickly gain control over all the resources in the network.

This allows the attacker to inflict major damage to the enterprise by stealing or modifying confidential data, disrupting daily operating procedures, upsetting financial transactions, slowing down network traffic, denying legitimate service to other users and diverting communication and sensitive data to offsite malicious servers.

WHAT IS THE BEST WAY TO MITIGATE THIS THREAT?

Use administrative privileges only when necessary. Introduce focused auditing on all persons who use the administrative privileges and monitor all anomalous behavior. Inventory all the administrative privileges using an automated tool, and validate that a senior executive has authorizedeach person who uses administrative privileges.

Change over all administrative passwords to be complex formations of intermixed special characters, numbers, letters and alphabets. Strong passwords of sufficient length make it difficult for the attacker to guess and to crack.

Passwords for administrators should be changed at frequent intervals. Any new device, when being introduced to the networked environment, must have all its default passwords changed to longer and relatively more difficult passwords.

Passwords for all systems must be stored in an encrypted format, only readable by those with super-user privileges. The control lists must ensure that administrative accounts are used only for activities requiring system administration and not for general activities such as reading e-mails.

REFERENCES:

1. The SANS Institute, *Critical Control 12: Controlled Use of Administrative Privileges*. Available from: <http://www.sans.org/critical-security-controls/control.php?id=12>. [2013].

2. Hau, D., *The SANS Institute, Unauthorized Access – Threats, Risk, and Control*. Available from: <http://www.giac.org/paper/gsec/3161/unauthorized-accessthreats-risk-control/105264>. [11 July 2013].

3. Computer Economica, *Security Threats in Employee Misuse of IT Resources*. Available from: <http://www.computereconomics.com/article.cfm?id=1436>. [March 2009].

12

CLOUD COMPUTING THREATS

WHAT THREATS ARE FACED BY CLOUD COMPUTING?

Compared with incidences of computer security that affect corporate systems in general, cloud service providers have faced relatively fewer attacks. This could be because the providers of cloud services have stronger security, as they are more concerned about the data breach and the reputational consequences that would ensue. In the world of cloud computing, threats could be faced at three levels – the service provider, the tenant or the user of the service, and the transmission path connecting the two.

Some of the security and crime risks that the providers of cloud services face are as follows:

- » Authentication issues

- » Denial of service attacks

- » Use of cloud computing for criminal activities

- » Illegal activities by the service provider

- » Attacks on physical security

- » Insider abuse of access

- » Malware

- » Cross-guest virtual machine breaches or side channel attacks

- » Insecure or obsolete encryption

- » Structured Query Language injection

Tenants of cloud computing may face security and crime risks of the following nature:

- » Phishing

- » Domain name system attacks

- » Compromising of the device accessing the cloud

- » Access management issues

Some attacks that target the transmission of data could be of the following nature:

- » Session hijacking and session riding

- » Man-in-the-middle attacks

- » Network/packet sniffing

When username and password combinations are obtained and used without authorization, it may lead to authentication issues on cloud systems. The information may have been obtained by various means, including guessing, keylogging malware, password recovery mechanisms or social engineering attacks.

Attackers can send a flood of traffic to overwhelm the websites, making them inaccessible to legitimate users. This type of denial of service is generally perpetrated using a botnet and causes widespread distributed denial of service or DDoS.

As the cloud services are meant for sharing resources, existing accounts may be compromised or new accounts may be created using stolen credit card details and credentials. This reduces the cost to the offenders, and makes it difficult to trace the source of the attack, especially when jurisdictions are crossed.

Providers of cloud services may themselves be involved in illegal activities such as piracy. When authorities close the services, all other users of the service suffer, as they are unable to access their documents.

Attackers are also known to have physically attacked the providers of cloud services, stealing hardware, and accessing servers without proper authorization causing loss of data.

Discontented employees of a cloud service provider are easy prey to attackers and may misuse their privileges to obtain access to stored data or disrupt access to legitimate users in lieu of potential perceived gains. More than 50% of the ICT7 professionals were concerned about insider threats in the cloud, including planting malware.

If the victim's and the attacker's virtual machines are both located on the same physical machine, there could be side channel attack. The attacker may access the data of the other tenants using the same physical resources.

Insecure or obsolete encryption may be another opportunity for attackers to read unauthorized data. Analyzing accessed positions and monitoring the query access pattern of the client may also lead to reading sensitive information.

Attackers may inject Structured Query Language code that performs erroneously in the database back end. This could lead to data access and possible modification without due authorization.

Phishing and DNS attacks are other threats that users of cloud services face. These may not be linked directly to the cloud service itself, but the user may be hijacked to use another resource masquerading as the authentic one and made to disgorge all his credentials.

PREVENTIVE MEASURES

According to the CSA or the Cloud Security Alliance, there is no single-shot solution to preventing or reducing the risk of threats to the security of cloud computing. Their recommendations include a defensive and in-depth strategy, which includes security enforcements for computing, storage, network, application and the user, as well as monitoring.

REFERENCES:

1. Gonsalves, A., *ReadWrite, The 9 Top Threats Facing Cloud Computing*. Available from: <http://readwrite.com/2013/03/04/9-top-threats-from-cloud-computing#awesm=~o8TDlRF1BuaCmO>. [4 March 2013].

2. Samson, T., *InfoWorld, 9 top threats to cloud computing security*. Available from: <http://www.infoworld.com/t/cloud-security/9-top-threats-cloud-computing-security-213428>. [25 February 2013].

3. Hutchings, A., Smith, R.G. & JamesL., Australian Institute of Criminology, *Cloud computing for small business: Criminal and security threats and prevention measures*. Available from: <http://www.aic.gov.au/publications/current%20series/tandi/441-460/tandi456.html>. [May 2013].

TARGETED BOTNET ATTACKS AND YOUR RESPONSE

Since 15 April 2013, more than 90,000 computers have together attacked the WordPress website hosted by Cloud-Flare and Hostgator. All users of WordPress, with username "admin" were targeted and more than 10 million random passwords were tried every minute to gain access to their accounts. This targeted attack of the botnets is one of the most powerful ever to be waged on WordPress.

WHAT ARE BOTNETS?

Cyber criminals infiltrate a computer by placing a malware inside it. That turns the computer into a bot, also called a drone or a zombie. The malware resides within the operating system, camouflaging itself from the anti-virus and antimalware security programs and multiplying itself whenever files from the infected computer are transferred to another computer, infecting the second computer as well. Very soon, it infects several computers in a row and connects all of them via the Internet to form a botnet, which then comes under the control of the botmaster.

HOW BOTNETS AFFECT COMPUTERS

Botnets use a coordinated brute force attack, flooding the targeted server with countless login requests. The botnets try various combinations of usernames and passwords to gain entry, and own the user's accounts they can break into. The attack usually slows down the servers and users on the server are locked out of their websites. This is called the DDoS or the Direct Denial of Service. As WordPress users are given a username "Admin" while they use a password of their own choice, the botnet that attacked the WordPress servers went after users who had not changed their original username.

Once a computer is compromised, it forms another bot and becomes a part of the botnet. The botmaster can extract any information from the compromised machine. Impressive numbers of computers in a targeted attack have the ability to inflict real damage. A single IP or a few IPs can be easily blocked out, but it becomes a different matter when a substantially large number of IPs (above 90,000 in the attack on WordPress) are involved. Attack from multiple computers can be timed to occur several times a second (trying as many as over two billion passwords an hour), overwhelming the security at the server they have targeted.

WHY DO BOTNETS ATTACK COMPUTER SERVERS?

Botnets are constantly trying to increase their numbers so that they can create the condition of an overwhelming flood when they attack. In their quest for adding more computers to their botnets, botmasters target servers with more users attached. Botmasters went after Wordpress as, unlike most home computers, servers hosting WordPress blogs are some of the best in processing power.

Any botmaster setting up a botnet seeks powerful computers. A botnet of such computers can be far more powerful than a regular home-computer constituted botnet, and can then launch DDoS attacks of far greater intensity than what is normally witnessed.

More than 60 million websites around the world are hosted on WordPress, and botmasters would have tremendous computing power if they were able to control even a fraction of these sites.

HOW CAN YOU PREVENT YOUR OWN SITE FROM BEING COMPROMISED BY BOTNETS?

Although the botnets use brute force to try to gain control, it is relatively easy to hold them off. In the case of WordPress users, they had to change their username from "admin" to something different, and at the same time, make their passwords stronger by using a combination of numbers, letters and special characters.

Use of two-step authentication can be another deterrent against botnet attacks. Although it increases the annoyance while logging on to sites like WordPress, it makes it easier for the servers to detect that you are not a bot before they log you on. This makes your site far more secure.

CloudFlare, the server that hosts WordPress, offers free plans that guarantee automatic block for any login attempt that looks like it is from a botnet.

Use the latest released version of the application, as Word- Press has already blocked security holes that attackers were exploiting.

REFERENCES:

1. BBC, News Technology, *WordPress website targeted by hackers.* Available from: <http://www.bbc.co.uk/news/technology-22152296>. [15 April 2013].

2. Wheately, M., siliconANGLE, *How To Sidestep The Word-Press Botnet Hack.* Available from: <http://siliconangle.com/blog/2013/04/15/how-to-sidestep-the-wordpress-botnet-hack/>. [15 April 2013].

3.   Vincent, J., *The Independent, $500 million botnet Citadel attacked by Microsoft and the FBI*. Available from:<http://www.independent.co.uk/life-style/gadgetsand-tech/news/500-million-botnet-citadel-attackedby-microsoft-and-the-fbi-8647594.html>. [6 June 2013].

14

STRATEGIC MALWARE DEFENSE

WHAT IS MALWARE?

Malware is malicious software that has now become a dangerous aspect and an integral part of threats from the Internet. Organizations and end-users become targets via browsing of the net, attachments to emails, using the cloud and other vectors including the mobile devices.

HOW MALWARE WORKS

Malicious software and code can tamper with and change the contents of a system. It can capture sensitive data while infecting other systems on the network. Modern malware has evolved beyond the behavioral and signature-based detection of most anti-virus tools and may have the capability to disable the tools monitoring the system. System administrators use Anti-malware tools, comprising antispyware and anti-virus tools to defend against the threats from malware.

EXTENT OF DAMAGE CAUSED BY MALWARE

Depending on the targets of the virus, the damage to an infected computer on a network can vary: from sending out spam, to a complete breakdown of the network or critical data loss.

Cost is one way of measuring the detrimental effects of malware. The cost to the global economy is as much as $1 trillion a year from cybercriminals using malware to steal personal data such as credit card information. That means the individual business must spend an average of $3.8 million in reacting to, containing, and cleaning up after a malware attack. Per incident, the average loss for a customer affected by malware works out to be about $1,000, and this figure excludes the fear and loss of trust that accompanies a cybercrime.

Malware lodged in your website can blacklist your site by search engines such as Google. It may take up to 13 days on average to be removed from the blacklist. During this time, customers see warnings that your site is unsafe, forcing them to move toward your competitor's business. That means nearly two weeks of lost sales because of decreased traffic.

Apart from the involvement of cost and loss in sales, malware attacks can be more damaging as the reputation of your business may be hit seriously. Even one lost potential customer (seeing the blacklist warning) may spread the word that your site (read business) cannot be trusted. With tools such as Twitter and Facebook, it takes only seconds for this mistrust to spread to thousands of people. Therefore, even if you were at best only a victim of malware attack, you risk losing sales and reputation.

BEST PRACTICES TO THWART MALWARE ATTACKS

Aside from taking a holistic approach for the overall security of the network, different classes of threats require different defenses. Specifically for malware, protection of the web-server is the predominant approach.

The latest trend is toward adding a protection layer that works at the website level. Anti-malware scanning from a cloud-based service is emerging as the most powerful and effective supplement to web server security implemented in the traditional manner.

The service conducts regular scans to detect hidden malware in web pages facing the customer and alerts the website owners if any malware is found. Features include changing scanning speed and frequency, using databases to keep track of threats, varying reporting capabilities, dynamic updates and integration with related tools.

REFERENCES:

1. The SANS Institute, *Twenty Critical Security Controls for Effective Cyber Defense*. Available from: <http://www.sans.org/critical-security-controls/>. [2013].

2. Kaspersky, *Damage caused by malware*. Available from: <http://www.securelist.com/en/threats/detect?chapter=76>. [1997].

3. Symantec, WHITE PAPER: *How Malware Infects Websites and Harms Businesses —and What You Can Do to Stop It*. Available from: <http://www.geotrust.com/anti-malware-scan/malware-threat-white-paper.pdf>. [2012].

15

DOS ATTACK SECURITY STRATEGIES

WHAT IS A DOS ATTACK?

Rogue attackers usually target web servers with intent to disrupt services. Users are prevented from connecting to the server for an online application or service, and this is commonly termed as denial of service or DOS. When multiple hosts are compromised in this manner, it is called DDOS or distributed denial of service.

Typical targets for a DOS attack are firewalls, routers, application servers, DNS servers and Web servers. Attackers create the DOS conditions by impairing the server itself or by consuming the bandwidth of the server.

As more companies conduct their businesses online, DOS/DDOS attacks are increasing, leading to severe losses in finance and productivity. The enormity of the problem can be judged by the Verisign survey of IT decision makers, which revealed that more than 60% of the respondents had sustained an attack of DOS in the past year, and more than 10% of these had been hit six or more times. More than 50% of those attacked reported downtime, which resulted in revenue loss.

REPERCUSSIONS OF A DOS ATTACK

The denial of service attack usually spans several entry points or vectors on the network simultaneously. Most often, attackers rope in multiple compromised PCs, which then act as zombies. Botnets or armies of zombie PCs then inject malware such as viruses, Trojans and spam into the network.

This activity multiplies into generating multiple gigabytesper- second of network traffic, creating large scale distributed denial of service, clogging the access network and denying service to legitimate users. As a consequence, business operations and revenue are severely undermined.

Apart from revenue loss and downtime, DOS attacks lead to devastating effects for many businesses. This usually takes the form of a downward plunge in brand reputation, bottom line and customer relationships. Times are changing, and attackers are resorting to advanced forms of DOS attacks. Most traditional approaches to counter such attacks with intrusion prevention system devices, firewalls and over-provisioning of bandwidth no longer work, leaving the services, applications and networks of an organization unprotected.

SOME USEFUL METHODS TO KEEP YOUR NETWORK SAFE FROM DOS ATTACKS

» Incorporate normal redundancy, use more servers spread around many datacenters, and use good load balancing;

» Lock down your DNS servers, use enhanced DNS protection, and similar load balancing as already in use for your web and other resources;

» Set up good firewalls, let routers drop junk packets and block ICMP;

» Plan to replace dynamic resources quickly with static ones.

Having more servers helps to spread the load, provided you have large pipes to handle all the traffic; as large as your financial resources will allow.

Even if your website is not being attacked, an attack on the DNS servers is as bad. If one is able to resolve your DNS name and connect to your DNS servers, they will be able to reach your website. That means your DNS servers must be protected with the same thoroughness as your other resources.

When you are managing your own network and serving your own data, you must take the protection to the network layer. For example, your website is never going to generate random queries to your DNS servers. Therefore, you may safely block all UDP port 53 packets from reaching your servers.

Despite the precautions, some attacks may filter through, and you must be prepared to mitigate the threat. Often the target of the attack is the database or some custom scripts you are running. Use of caching servers and providing static content can help if you are under attack.

REFERENCES:

1. Verisign, *What Is a DDoS Attack?* Available from: <http://www.verisigninc.com/en_US/products-and-services/network-intelligence-availability/ddos/ddos-attack/index.xhtml>. [2011].

2. AT&T, *Denial of Service - DDoS Protection.* Available from: <http://www.business.att.com/enterprise/Service/network-security/threat-vulnerability-management/ddos-protection/>. [29 June 2013].

3. Lambert, P., TechRepublic, *DDoS attack methods and how to prevent or mitigate them.* Available from: <http://www.techrepublic.com/blog/security/ddos-attack-methods-and-how-to-prevent-or-mitigate-them/8523>. [15October 2012].

16

YOU NEED PATCH MANAGEMENT

WHAT IS PATCH MANAGEMENT?

One major time-consumer in business is to keep the infrastructure functional. For most businesses, the IT department spends more than 70% of its time in maintenance and administration, according to recent research from the International Data Corporation (IDC). For some, this figure is even higher, reaching 80% or more.

Updating, maintaining and patching software and systems for the latest security vulnerabilities are now major overhead expenses for IT managers. This is because IT systems are now more complex and distributed, and there is a significant increase in the overhead costs involved in keeping the systems functioning smoothly.

Software manufacturers release patch updates frequently, depending on how fast they are able to overcome vulnerabilities found in their programs. Not only software, but now firmware, development systems and hardware manufacturers also produce updates, and there are patches from software vendors and out-of-band patches to be handled.

WHY SHOULD PATCH MANAGEMENT BE A PRIORITY?

Most business' networks could carry a flaw in their unpatched systems, representing a real security threat. According to the US technology standards body, the NIST, in more than 90% of successful attacks against companies, the attackers exploited vulnerabilities that were already known. All the attacks could have been prevented had the systems been patched correctly and in time.

HOW SHOULD PATCH MANAGEMENT BE HANDLED?

IT departments in a business may decide to let users handle their own patch updates to reduce the company's IT burden. The real situation is not all patches released by their manufacturers install without creating further problems. There is risk of a breakup of critical business processes when users patch their systems with an untested patch. While off-the-shelf software is capable of being thus disrupted, it is more common with highly customized in-house software.

Centralized methods for patch management are therefore quickly catching up with businesses. For large businesses, the sheer numbers of servers, desktop systems, smartphones, tablets and all associated applications make it almost impossible to patch all devices manually. Automated systems of patch management handle such situations with more reliability and increased security.

Automated patch management can take care of the growing number of threats built specifically to attack systems before they are upgraded or patched. Many businesses and their IT security focus on mitigating the zero-day exploits, but human error in manual patching leaves too many systems vulnerable, even long after the patches have been released.

Manual and uncoordinated patching can leave the enterprise in a state of disruption and cause loss through downtime. This is mostly true in the case of patches untested for their compatibility with the operating software.

WHY AUTOMATED PATCHING IS AN ADVANTAGE TO BUSINESSES

Enterprises must implement in-house testing or look at using a patch supplier who also handles testing before applying patches on running systems. Although it does increase patch management cost deployment, the benefits far outweigh the investments due to the reduction in downtime and the consequent lost revenue.

Using automated patch management, the enterprise remains productive and conserves valuable IT resources. Most automated patch management systems can be programmed to implement patching beyond the core working time.

REFERENCES:

1. Lutz, S. *Help Net Security, Automate your way out of patching hell.* Available from: <http://www.net-security.org/article.php?id=1845>. [30 May 2013].

2. Florian, C., *TechTalkToMe, 5 Benefits of Automating Patch Management.* Available from: <http://www.gfi.com/blog/5-benefits-automating-patch-management/>. [25November 2010].

3. Symantec, *Automatic Patch Management.* Available from: <http://www.symantec.com/articles/article.jsp?aid=automating_patch_management>. [8 February,2005].

17

MAINTAINING, MONITORING AND ANALYZING

WHAT HAPPENS WITHOUT LOGGING OF AUDIT RECORDS?

Audit logs provide clues that allow administrators to follow the trails of attackers within an enterprise's compromised network system. Any deficiency in the logging and analysis of the security logs allows the attackers to hide the location of their malicious software and use it to control and monitor activities on the victim's machine.

Even when an attack on the victim's machine is established with certainty, the complete details of the attack and the extent of damage can only be known by studying the complete logging records, provided they have been protected from damage. However, in the absence of solid logs, not only will such attacks go unnoticed for long periods, but also the damage done may well be irreversible.

Attackers using smart technologies can erase their trail effectively. Sometimes the only way to detect such attacks is through analysis of the logging records. Organizations who keep the logs for compliance alone, may not glance at the audit logs, and therefore, may never know when their systems have been comprised, even when the traces of the attack are evident in the unexamined log files.

HOW DOES LACK OF AUDIT LOGS AFFECT THE ORGANIZATION?

With absence of audit logs, an enterprise will be unable to achieve several security-related objectives such as:

> » Individual accountability

> » Reconstruction of events

> » Intrusion detection

> » Problem analysis

Audit trails work in tandem with logical access control, as this restricts the use of system resources. This allows monitoring of users suspected of improperly modifying data or introducing errors within a database. The audit trail establishes the "before" and "after" versions of the records. Without the audit trail, it is impossible to establish who made the errors, whether it was the user, the system, the application software or an external attacker.

Audit trails are useful for reconstructing events once a problem has been detected. System logs can pinpoint the exact system activity that led to the cessation of normal operations. For example, with the help of an analysis of the audit trail, it is easy to distinguish between errors induced by operators and errors created by the system.

Logged activities can identify attempts at penetrating a system to gain unauthorized access. However, absence of logging or failure to analyze the existing logs can lead to external attackers gaining access to the network.

HOW CAN THIS THREAT BE MITIGATED?

Use both types of audit records and record them – an event oriented log and keystroke monitoring. Set event based logs to record system events, application events, and user events.

Set the audit trail to include sufficient information, establishing what events occurred and who caused them. For keystroke monitoring, preserve keystrokes along with user identification, as this will enable administrators to determine which specific user entered the keystrokes.

Use at least two synchronized time sources or Network Time Protocol (NTP), and use them on all servers and network equipment. Use the same time stamp for logs as well, so that there is consistency throughout the network.

REFERENCES:

1. The SANS Institute, *Critical Control 14: Maintenance, Monitoring, and Analysis of Audit Logs*. Available from: <http://www.sans.org/critical-security-controls/control.php?id=14>. [2012].

2. NIST Special Publication 800-12, *Introduction to Computer Security: The NIST Handbook*. Available from: <http://csrc.nist.gov/publications/nistbul/itl97-03.txt>. [2012].

3. *ThreatTrack Security Inc.* Available from: <http://www.threattracksecurity.com/documents/enterprisesecurity-white-paper-sandboxing-helps-avoid-security-breach.pdf>. [2012].

18

WHAT IS A BANK AND WHAT DOES IT DO?

If you have $1,000 that you don't need right away, but you want to earn more money – interest – on that $1,000, you deposit the money in the bank. The bank pays you to hold your money. When you put money in the bank, it is called a deposit. When the bank pays you to hold your money, it is called "interest."

The bank also lends money, and when it does, it collects interest. If you want to buy a go-cart that costs $500 but you don't have that much, you can ask the bank to lend you the money. If you have a way to pay the bank back, the bank will lend you the money and it will charge you interest.

This is how banks make money and can afford to pay you interest on your deposit. The interest the bank pays you is less than the interest it collects from the person who borrowed money. This means that if you deposit $1,000 and the bank pays you 5 percent interest, which is $50 dollars per month, every month your balance – the amount you have in your bank account – goes up. After the first month, you will have $1,050 in the bank. After the second month, you will have $1,102.50.

Now, if another person borrows $500, the bank might charge that person 10 percent per month. This means that the person who borrowed the money has to pay back the $500 plus $50 the first month. If the payment on the $500 is only $25, the next month the person who borrowed the money will owe $475 plus 10 percent interest, which means his payment would be $72.50: $25 plus 10 percent of $475. The bank is making a lot of money so has some to pay you interest on your deposit, plus some extra, which is called "profit."

The bank uses profits to pay the people who work there, the rent on the bank building and to pay for electricity, telephones and other bills.

WHERE DOES MY MONEY GO?

When you make a deposit, the bank teller puts the money with everyone else's money. The teller enters the amount you gave him into the computer to keep track of how much of that money belongs to you. This is called your balance. Your balance goes up when you add more money and goes down when you take money out of the bank. The bank uses everyone's money to make loans to people who want to borrow money.

WHY DO PEOPLE BORROW MONEY FROM THE BANK?

In most cases, people can't borrow money from their parents or from friends or even a stranger because those people might not have that much money. Plus, how would those people know they would get their money back? That is part of what banks do – they hold your money and they lend money to people who want to buy something that costs a lot. It is also how the bank makes money to pay the people who work there.

HOW ELSE DO BANKS MAKE MONEY?

Not everyone needs to borrow money all the time; and not everyone can afford to borrow money. If a person does not go to work every day, the bank will not let that person borrow money because he has no way to pay it back. When banks do lend money, it takes a long time to get the money back because people pay it back a little at a time – in payments. Because of this the bank has to have another way to make money. Banks charge the people who deposit money a bank fee to use the bank's services. If you have a checking account – a place to store your money until you need it to pay bills – the bank might charge you a little bit every month to help pay the bank's bills. This is called a bank fee.

WHO CAN DEPOSIT MONEY IN THE BANK?

Any person or company that has a bank account can deposit money in the bank. Big companies deposit lots of money when they sell things. When you go to the fair and have to pay money to get in, the people at the fair deposit the money in their bank. That money is used to pay people who work at the fair and for the electricity the fair needs to make the rides work. It is also used to buy some of the ingredients needed to make that wonderful cotton candy and funnel cakes that you can buy at the fair.

Since a lot of people go to the fair, the fair collects a lot of money. To keep the money safe and to make it easier to pay people to keep the fair running, all that money is deposited in the bank. This is also how banks can lend money to people who need it – because big companies and people with a lot of money keep their money in the bank.

WHAT IS BETTER: A CHECKING OR SAVINGS ACCOUNT?

This depends on how you want to use the money. If you have bills to pay every month, it is better to have a checking account because your money is always there for you to use. If you don't need your money for a long time, you might decide to put it in a savings account. Some banks tell you that if you put your money in a savings account, you can't use it for some time. Sometimes that might be for a few months, or it could be a year or longer.

Even though you cannot use that money right away, it is earning you extra money. Because the bank is holding your money and lending it to other people, it must pay you. The bank pays you in the form of interest.

MORE ABOUT MAKING LOANS?

You may be thinking that you might need your money and are wondering how you will get it if the bank lent it to someone else. Most of the time, a person who deposits money into a savings account does not need his money right away. Because of this, banks can use deposits from a lot of people – these are called short-term deposits because the bank knows that you will eventually need your money – to make long-term loans.

It takes people longer to pay the bank back, but during that time, other people keep making deposits. Plus – don't forget – the bank makes money on fees that it charges for people to use the bank to store money; and it makes money on interest that it charges people to borrow money. This process is called maturity transformation. When a bank makes a loan, it is called an asset because the person who borrowed the money has to pay it back.

Most of the money the bank makes comes from interest it collects on the money it loaned to other people. Another way banks make money is to give or issue securities. These are usually commercial paper or bonds. The bank owns these securities and can lend them out to other banks in exchange for cash money. The bank uses the cash money to pay you for your deposit and to pay other things like bills and the people who work at the bank.

When a bank does this, it must pay interest to the bank who lent them the cash. The other bank makes money. Securities are another form of savings. When a bank trades cash money for another bank's securities, it also makes money on the loan. These types of "trades" or transactions are called "repurchase agreements."

A bank can also sell their loans. This is often referred to as "selling paper." When a bank makes a loan for a house, the person who borrowed the money has to sign a mortgage. This is an agreement between the person who borrowed the money and the bank; and it shows that the person who borrowed the money has to pay it back to the bank.

The bank takes many mortgages and adds them together. If 50 different people borrowed $100,000 to buy houses that means that the bank is owed $5,000,000. This is another asset – something the bank owns. The money is not in the bank's vault, but in an agreement stating that each person owes the bank.

The bank can bundle the mortgages together and sell them at a discount rate to another bank so it can have most of the cash back right away. The bank might sell $5,000,000 in mortgages to another bank for $4,000,000. The bank who bought the mortgages pays the bank who is selling them $4,000,000. The bank that paid the cash collects the money from the people who borrowed the money. If everyone pays their mortgage, the new bank will make $1,000,000 plus the interest.

The bank that got the cash in exchange for the mortgages can use the money to lend to other people. The bank will charge an interest rate high enough to make the $1,000,000 it lost by selling the mortgages at a discount, plus a little more profit. This process is called "liquidity transformation and securitization."

BANK TRANSACTIONS

Banks not only allow you to save and borrow money, but they also create money with a "domestic and international payments system." If you deposit money into a checking account, you have to be able to use that money to pay other people. You may want to buy groceries, pay the light bill or you may need to make a house payment. Another part of this is when you work, you get paid for the work you do for someone.

The banks process the payments needed for people to live life. Your boss puts money into the bank when he sells something. He has to pay you for working for him, so he transfers some of that money to you. He can do that by writing you a check or by transferring the money by way of an electronic transaction. A check is a piece of paper that says someone owes you money. When you take the check to the bank, the bank subtracts the amount from your boss's account and adds it to your account.

You can pay your bills the same way. After you earn money and your boss gives you a check or makes an electronic deposit to your account, you can use the money to pay your bills or to buy groceries. You can write a check or pay by debit card. You can even go to the bank and take money out and give cash to the grocery store when you buy groceries. If you were to write a check for groceries, the grocery store would deposit the check. The store's bank adds money to the store's bank account and subtracts it from your bank account.

If something were to happen to the payment system, people could not pay bills. If your boss cannot pay you because the bank's payment system is not working properly, then you won't be able to buy groceries. The ability to buy goods and services is called trade. If the payment system is not working, people cannot trade things for money and the economic growth – the amount people in general spend – does not grow as fast. This means that everyone suffers because there may be shortages on food, gas and other things that people need to live.

OTHER WAYS BANKS CAN CREATE MONEY

Banks are not allowed to lend out all the money people deposit. They must keep some; and this is called "reserves." The bank can hold reserves in the form of cash money or securities – securities can be easily converted to cash money. The bank figures out how much money people take out of their savings and checking accounts.

It also has rules it has to follow. A "central bank," or in the case of banks in the United States, the Federal Reserve Bank, tells banks how much money they have to keep in the bank. This means that if you deposit $1,000, the bank cannot use all of your money – it can only use some of your money so that it has money ready to give you when you are ready to take your money out to buy something.

A bank can also sell insurance and mutual funds to raise money. Another thing that is tied into mortgages is loan servicing. A bank can charge a person who borrows money to take care of the loan. This is called loan servicing. In this process, the bank collects money from the person who borrowed money and adjusts the borrower's balance when the borrower pays every month.

A bank can agree with another bank or company to service their loans. If this is the case, the bank collects the payments from people who borrowed money, then sends the money to the other bank or company. The bank that is collecting the money charges the other bank or company a fee to collect money.

TRANSMITTING MONETARY POLICY

When the economy grows, everyone makes money. This could – in some circumstances -- cause inflation. Inflation is the amount prices rise compared against the amount of money people make (purchasing power). If inflation goes up 2 percent, that means that the candy you paid $1 for today will cost $1.02 next year.

Banks control all of the money. The central bank controls the money throughout the nation, but local banks can also control money. The central bank can change the rules and tell your bank how much money it has to keep in reserves. If the amount is higher than it was before the central bank changed the rules, that means the local bank has less money to lend.

When a bank has less money to lend, it charges more interest to people who want to borrow the money. A local bank can also decide to put more of its deposits into the reserves. If the central bank or a local bank decides to put too much money in reserves and there is less money to loan people, the nation suffers a "credit crunch." That is because there isn't enough money to lend. This is when the cost of borrowing money goes up.

If people can't borrow money then they can't buy expensive things like new cars and houses. If your neighbor lost his job and can't pay for his house, he would have to sell his house. But if the banks are not lending money, he won't be able to sell the house because no one will be able to get the loan to buy the house.

This means that the neighbor can't sell his house and he can't make the house payment, so the bank takes the house. Now the bank has a house that it can't move into – because banks don't set up shop in houses – and no cash because the person who borrowed the money can't buy it back and because another person can't buy it since the banks don't have the money to lend to other people. This is one of the most common ways to hurt the economy.

When the economy fails, banks can also fail. If people who deposit money in the bank no longer trust the bank, they will take all of their money out of the bank. Since the bank lends out some of the money, it can't afford to pay every person his money. This is how a bank fails. The FDIC insures the people's money in the event that something like this happens, but it only insures $100,000. If you have $200,000 in the same bank, you will only get $100,000 of that money if the bank fails before you can get your money out.

Banks can also fail because it has more checking accounts than other sources of income and because it doesn't have a lot of cash, but has a lot of assets. Not all assets can be turned into cash (sold) right away. This means a bank could be rich because of the assets it owns, but it doesn't have any cash money to give to people who hold accounts at the bank.

BANK REGULATION

The rules that banks must follow are designed to keep banks from failing – in most cases. If a bank fails, people tend to panic and withdraw their money, causing a bad situation to become worse.

A bank can take an emergency loan from the central bank if it has to so that it doesn't fail. Most countries also require a bank to have a charter. A charter is how a bank is formed and it contains the rules that the bank must follow. A bank must also insure its deposits up to a certain amount. In the United States, that amount is $100,000 per bank account.

If a bank does business in another country, they must also follow that country's banking rules. The rules also state that banks cannot do certain things as far as credit and the market go. A bank cannot invest in companies or people with bad credit – people who don't pay their bills. A bank must also keep more of their profits just like you would keep your money in a savings account.

If the bank is going to fail, then it has some savings to help it survive until it gets back on its feet. This is called "capital." Banks that operate in many countries have to have more capital than local banks. A bank must also keep a certain amount of liquid assets such as securities. Liquid assets are those that can be sold immediately for cash.

SUMMARY

If you want to save up for something special, you can open a bank account with your parents. This is a good way to learn how to save money early and how to manage a bank account. Ask your parents to help you open a savings account that pays interest. Put part of your allowance in the bank account. Once you get older and start babysitting or mowing lawns, you can add some of that money to the bank account.

19

THE EFFECTS OF BLENDED THREATS AND JAVASCRIPT

WHAT IS A BLENDED THREAT AND JAVASCRIPT?

A blended threat is a single threat that carries multiple vectors inside to cause further damage. A malicious JavaScript containing multiple malware, Trojans, etc. within, can hijack a web browser and exploit further vulnerabilities inside. The multiple vectors may target the host, disable the security software and download more worms, Trojans and backdoors. These could be used to further control the now hijacked machine, such as sending out spam and hosting web pages to cause further damage.

WHAT HAPPENS DURING A BLENDED THREAT ATTACK?

We have all visited free download sites that make us wait, say 30 seconds before the download starts, counting down as 29, 28, 27, etc. An attacker can couch his attack in a similar way and during the waiting time, change the password to the router, or upload new firmware. This allows the attacker to do whatever he wishes. Usually, this is sniffing the traffic for passwords and similar information, and forwarding them to the attacker's site.

A JavaScript attack blends cross-site scripting in a known application with vulnerabilities in application cookie security. This can also happen by exploiting human trust, requiring a user to enter their credentials into a malicious web page that is designed to mimic the original application.

With a successful attack, the attacker can gain access to sensitive information and or privilege escalation through additional vulnerabilities. The attacker can change the configuration of a device or the password of the administrator as well.

The attacker begins his attack on the internal networks by inducing the user to run a small JavaScript code initiated through the browser. Several different vectors may be used for this, for example, sites offering surveys, malicious Search Engine Optimization, social networks, media download sites and compromised ad networks.

A blended attack may also be used to discover the devices existing on the victim's network, and exploiting the vulnerabilities. The attacker can then achieve a persistent and most often a permanent network compromise.

To achieve a level of persistence, in which the attacker maintains access to a compromised device over long periods, the attacker may use C&C or botnet Command and Control systems.

Attackers mainly target Small Office Home Office (SOHO) routers since this affords them additional benefits. One of the benefits is the target is directly addressable from the Internet. The attacker can then implement port-knocking techniques to sniff for pre-determined sequence of packets.

WHAT ARE THE RISKS FROM A BLENDED THREAT ATTACK?

With a permanent presence in a network, a whole world of possibilities opens up for the attacker. The level of functionality gained after exploiting the network gives some idea of the extent of damage that is possible in the attack:

- » Sniffing for passwords and credit card details
- » Intercepting the network and replacing ad-network engines
- » Pivoting on the network to attack other devices
- » Propagating to other local networks and foreign networks
- » Denial of service for completely covert attacks
- » Creating scalable bot-nets with the routers
- » Creating a private VPN for the attacker
- » Intercepting/manipulating traffic
- » Inserting malicious JavaScript code to exploit further
- » Poisoning the cache
- » Attacking CDMA routers using JavaScript
- » Remote dialing modems or cellular enabled routers

HOW CAN RISKS FROM BLENDED THREAT ATTACKS BE MITIGATED?

- » Follow RFC-5735 and do not allow sites from the Internet to be able to access Private IP Addresses.
- » Restrict Cross-Origin Resource Sharing for transferring large chunks of data to foreign domains
- » Enable Cross Site Request Forgery protections on all embedded devices.
- » Use embedded devices that support secure and automatic software updates.
- » Limit the use of JavaScript in the enterprise as far as possible.
- » Establish new heuristics to detect and respond to blended JavaScript and CSFU threats.

REFERENCES:

1. Appsec Conulting Inc., *Blended Threats and JavaScript: A Plan for Permanent Network Compromise.* Available from: <http://media.blackhat.com/bh-us-12/Briefings/Purviance/BH_US_12_Purviance_Blended_Threats_WP.pdf>. [1 July, 2012].

2. Kyukendall, D., *Blended Threats & JavaScript (OWASP AppSecUSA Presentation Review).* Available from: <http://www.manvswebapp.com/blended-threats-javascriptplan-permanent-network-compromise>. [2013].

3. Fireeye, *Unraveling Web Malware.* Available from: <http://www.sarrelgroup.com/Documents/FE_unravel_web_malware_wp.pdf>. [2008].

20

WHAT IS A BLANK-CHECK COMPANY?

A blank check company is a development stage company that has no definite business plan or purpose or has laid out its business plan to connect in a merger or acquisition with an unidentified company or companies, other entity, or person. These companies in general involve tentative investments and come under the SEC's definition of "penny stocks" or "microcap stocks".

The companies are called the blank-check companies because this is what they get from the investors—a blank check for the company to select any (or no) targets for take-over. Since this is a blind-faith gesture, investor confidence depends on the status of the company principals.

The SEC prohibits the blank-check companies to use some of the exemptions from the registration requirement when selling their securities. The Security and exchange commission do so because of the nature of the blank-check companies.

If a blank check company registers for the security offering it should comply with some additional requirements for the protection of the investors, including depositing most of the raised funds in an escrow account until an acquisition is settled, and it requires shareholder approval of any identified acquisition.

"Special purpose Acquisition Company or SPAC" is a type of Blank Check Company. A SPAC is established specifically to raise funds in order to finance a merger or acquisition opportunity within a limited time period.

The Securities exchange commission has laid out some rules for the blank-check companies. At least 80% of the total shareholders' money should be utilized in all the acquisitions, and each acquisition is subjected to shareholder approval. If the company fails to find or execute at least one transaction by a given date (generally two years from inception), the funds plus accrued interest less operating expenses are returned to the shareholders.

Most of the blank-check companies issue initial public offerings of around 10 per share, but they can also raise funds without the approval of shareholders by issuing other class of stocks. So many companies do this to keep them safe from hostile takeover. Some of these companies have more than one class of preferred stock, and it's not easy if not impossible to differentiate one from the other. One of the major problems which arise in researching such area is that there is little to no information on the blank-checks which very well explains their thin trading volume.

There are about sixty to hundred blank-check companies trading on the US exchanges. The major player's, trade on AMEX.

The Blank check companies can succeed in for what they have been formed only when all hopes turn out into the final result. Management should be able to find an appropriate acquisition candidate and settle a bargain price. Operators must run the enterprise well. The stock market must shore up a rising valuation for the acquired company. But these factors seldom coincide.

Generally among all the factors one or two go wrong. Either the company fails to find a willing target and returns the money to investors or if everything goes on the track at times the company overpays for the acquisition, leaving IPO investors with big losses.

Since 2003, a total of 98 U.S. companies were set up to form such special-purpose acquisitions, according to SPAC Investments Ltd. The average annualized return of such so-called SPACs has been negative 18.4% in the stock market since 2003, against an average of 6.7 percent for the Standard & Poor's 500 Index.

The past records of the blank-check companies are full of scandals, and U.S. regulators have time after time made tougher rules on how these businesses operate. One of the rules says that the acquisitions can't advance without shareholders consent. Managers are prohibited from paying themselves huge and excessive fee before they have done any work or gamble away IPO earnings in ways that shareholders wouldn't welcome. These rules safeguard the U.S. investors to a large extent and should also be followed by other countries'.

In order to regulate the blank check company in the most effective way, such offerings should be off-limit to anyone except to the sorts of wealthy investors who by now participate in hedge funds and private equity. These kinds of rules will be important and efficient to safeguard the blank-check deals that allow perilous foreign companies to trade on U.S. or European exchanges without fulfilling usual listing requirements.

Global capital markets already make available ample of different ways for the best corporate acquirers to pursue their craft. At a time when more transparency and disclosure are critical to rejuvenate public confidence in the markets, the intrinsically opaque nature of the blank-check companies strikes a dissonant note.

21

ONLINE FRAUD AND MONEY MULE RISKS

On the Internet, there are plenty of job vacancies for a `Money Transfer Agent'. People also receive emails asking for help to transfer huge quantities of money from one country to another. The overabundance makes one wonder about the genuine nature of these offers, and causes many job seekers to be suspicious.

WHAT ARE ON-LINE FRAUDS AND MONEY MULES?

The sad fact is most of these online job offers are frauds and could lead to an inadvertent criminal record. It could also lead to an exclusion from the banking system for the naïve job seeker who is drawn to such illegal activities.

The online job seeker is often used as an unwitting 'money mule' and led to misusing their bank account by laundering money through their account. In 2012, the second most identified fraud was through misuse of bank accounts. More than 45,000 confirmed instances of such fraud were identified and several of them bore the hallmark of such 'money mule' activity.

Usually fraudsters use the money from illegal activities such as fake lotteries, boiler room frauds, drug dealing and investments, prostitution and people trafficking in such frauds. They try to push 'dirty money' through in an effort to make it appear 'clean'. Legally, accounts that are utilized to launder money must be closed and international regulators fine them heavily for failure to do so.

THE RISKS PEOPLE FACE FROM ONLINE FRAUDS AND MONEY MULES

You are at a risk of becoming a victim of online fraud, should you lose your personal information to others. You and your family may face threats and be forced to perform online fraud. Different types of online frauds are:

» Phishing – Fraud websites decked up to masquerade as genuine sites to steal usernames, passwords and banking information.

» Money Mules – Lucrative fraudulent jobs offered to young adults and teens luring them into money laundering activities.

» Online Bank Fraud – Numerous people bank online considering the convenience. Online banking poses security risks involving Worms, Trojan Horses, imposter websites and fake e-mails, threatening to steal your credentials with each online transaction and purchase.

HOW DO MONEY MULES WORK?

Fraudsters usually contact their prospective victims or money mules with advertisements for jobs via job search websites, Internet chat rooms or spam e-mails. They advertise the jobs as financial management work, adding that special knowledge for the job is unnecessary. Some fraudsters may also ask the mules to sign some official looking employment contracts.

Mules, once recruited, will receive funds into their accounts, most of them stolen from other compromised accounts. Mules will then be asked to take out the funds and forward them to overseas accounts typically using wire transfer services. For their services, they will receive a commission payment. With their account being involved in the money laundering transaction, the mule also becomes an unwitting participant in the frauds.

HOW TO PROTECT YOURSELF FROM MONEY MULE FRAUDS

Carefully inspect any unsolicited opportunity or offer to make easy money before you part with your personal information. Most of the frauds will be from overseas companies and it will be difficult for you to find out if they are authentic.

People phishing for information may replicate the website of a genuine company to entice you into their folds. They may even register a similar looking web address that adds authenticity to the fraud. However, there will be subtle differences in the website URLs and web addresses and you must be extremely careful and alert to be able to detect the differences.

One simple way to ascertain the genuineness of such offers is to call the company who has purportedly placed the ads. By searching for and visiting the home page of the company, you will be able to find out their contact details. Contact them with reference to the advertisement and you will immediately know if they are genuinely recruiting people.

REFERENCES:

1. CIFAS, *Beware Job Ads for Money Transfer Agents warns CIFAS*. Available from: <http://www.cifas.org.uk/moneymulescams_feb>. [26 February 2013].

2. ICICI Bank, *Money Mule*. Available from: <http://www.icicibank. com/online-safe-banking/beware-of-fraud/money-mule.html>. [2013].

3. eBay, *What Risks Do You Face From Online Fraud? Money Mules.* Available from: <http://www.ebay.co.uk/gds/What-Risks-Do-You-Face-From-Online-Fraud-Money-Mules/10000000006003964/g.html>. [2013].

22

INS AND OUTS OF CAPTCHA RE-RIDING ATTACKS

WHAT IS A CAPTCHA RE-RIDING ATTACK?

Many web sites want to distinguish whether it is a robot that is reading the site or a human, mostly to avoid the spread of spam. They use a system called CAPTCHA, which is an acronym for Completely Automated Public Turing Test to tell Computers and Humans Apart. The website has distorted text on the page, which can only be read by humans.

There are two types of CAPTCHA, one with a single word and one with two words. They mostly use old type fonts with deliberately introduced distortions to make it almost impossible for any OCR (Optical Character Recognition) to recognize. Therefore any automated system will not be able to bypass the CAPTCHA test. Websites use CAPTCHA when they want to avoid bogus memberships or hoax accounts. Some of the money related websites use it when creating new accounts. Some websites may test you with a CAPTCHA if you have entered a wrong password two or three times.

Attackers use the CAPTCHA re-riding attack to bypass the CAPTCHA protection, which the web applications adapt. In an HTTP session, the code for verifying the CAPTCHA solution sent by the user does not clear it; the attackers may exploit the situation. They use the same CAPTCHA solution to repeatedly send requests to the website.

WHAT HAPPENS DURING A CAPTCHA RE-RIDING ATTACK?

When a user visits a webpage and requests a registration the website creates an HTTP session, assigns it a session ID, and presents the registration page to the user along with the session ID inside a cookie. The registration page also has a tag, which directs the visitor's browser to a remote server to retrieve a CAPTCHA to be displayed on the screen.

The visitor's browser follows the instructions in the tag and sends a request to the remote server for the CAPTCHA. Accordingly, the server creates a new CAPTCHA with a random text and its solution, stores it for the current HTTP session and sends out the CAPTCHA image to the requesting client browser, to be displayed there.

The user solves the CAPTCHA and the browser sends the solution to the server for verification. The server retrieves its own solution from the HTTP session and verifies the solution with that provided by the client.

If the two solutions match, the client is given the clearance to proceed to the next logical step in the registration process; if the visitor's response doesn't match the CAPTCHA image, the registration process starts afresh.

During the verification process, the CAPTCHA solution remains inside the HTTP session and it is not cleared for as long as the session is alive. This is true if the verification succeeds and the user is cleared to the next step. If the verification fails, the web applications continue to use the same session ID and the same HTTP session. The attacker exploits this situation.

The attacker can solve the CAPTCHA and send the solution to the website, recording the submission using a web proxy. Using a custom script, or a tool such as Burp Intruder, he can send this request multiple times. With each request, he changes the User ID and is able to create multiple new accounts using the same single CAPTCHA solution, thus defeating the very purpose of having the CAPTCHA in the first place.

Instead of directly using them, attackers are exploiting the vulnerabilities to provide tools and data to others for illegal activities. Using such attacks, millions of harvested emails are often put up for sale, and these contain data related to military, government and intelligence agencies.

HOW TO PREVENT A CAPTCHA RE-RIDING ATTACK

Two major steps can prevent CAPTCHA re-riding attacks:

- » Never trust emails from unknown recipients offering something you did not request and demanding your information;

- » Reset the CAPTCHA solution within the HTTP session as soon as the CAPTCHA verification stage completes.

REFERENCES:

1. Kalra, G. S., *Open Security Research, CAPTCHA Re-Riding Attack.* Available from: <http://blog.opensecurityresearch.com/2012/02/captcha-re-riding-attack.html>.[28 February 2012].

2. Paganini, P., *Security Affairs, The offer of Russian underground for phishing campaigns.* Available from: <http://securityaffairs.co/wordpress/12756/cyber-crime/theoffer-of-russian-underground-for-phishing-campaigns.html>. [9 March 2013].

3. Kalra, G. S., *Blackhat.com, Bypassing CAPTCHAs by Impersonating CAPTCHA Providers.* Available from: <https://media.blackhat.com/bh-us-12/Arsenal/Kalra/BH_US_12_Kalra_Bypassing_CAPTCHAs_by_Impersonating_CAPTCHA_Providers_WP.pdf>. [28 February2012].

23

MAINTAINING AN INVENTORY OF ALL AUTHORIZED AND UNAUTHORIZED DEVICES

Meta Description: *Any system, including test systems connected to the network for even a short period, may become a relay point for causing damage to an organization.*

NATURE OF THE VULNERABILITY

Several rogue nation-states and groups today employ systems to continuously scan the address spaces of organizations they target. They wait and attack any new and unprotected systems that are attached to the network, including test systems. Anything such as a laptop or a PDA, not up to date with patches could be their target. It is easy for any attacker anywhere in the world to find and exploit such systems via the Internet.

Once the attackers have gained internal access, they could quickly find and compromise other such improperly secured computer systems on the network. The local nighttime window is most favored by the attackers to install backdoors into systems before they are hardened the next day.

With advancement of new technology, organizations allow employees to Bring Your Own Devices or BYOD to workplaces, where they are connected to the network of the organization. Many of these devices may already be compromised, and they can be used as a relay point to inflict damage to the organization.

EFFECT ON THE ORGANIZATION

If compromised and exploited, such vulnerability could result in:

- » Unauthorized disclosure of data
- » Sensitive data, relating to purchase, accounts, inventory, Intellectual Property, resources, marketing and sales may be revealed.
- » Unauthorized modification to the system, its data, or both
- » Denial of service, access to data, or both to authorized users

Attackers may permanently lock an exploited system to its compromised state, thereby assuring a permanent entry point into the organization every time the system is used. Without a proper inventory control of the hardware and software devices used on the network, an organization will have no way of knowing the entry point of the attackers.

Similar to locking up an exploited system, attackers may disallow authorized users from accessing service and data. Passwords may be changed and an authorized user may find he is unable to login into his bank account or a CEO unable to access the latest sales projections for the upcoming AGM.

HOW TO MITIGATE THE THREAT

Set up operational rules to make sure users in the organization are running only approved and licensed software on their machines. This has an additional benefit of tracking both under-utilized and over-deployed software licenses, since both issues are financially important to the organization.

Use appropriate software to provide constant automation for asset inventory discovery that will provide New MAC and New Host found alerts, whenever a new device is plugged into the network. Encouraging the use of a standard naming convention for all hosts on the network makes it easy to detect the unauthorized one standing out.

Separate virtual local area networks or VLANs may be created for untrusted devices such as BYOD systems.

Use automated tools to notify security about an unauthorized asset plugged into the network, within two minutes; achieve isolation within five minutes.

REFERENCES:

1. The SANS Institute, *Critical Control 10: Secure Configurations for Network Devices such as Firewalls, Routers, and Switches.* Available from: <http://www.sans.org/critical-security-controls/control. php?id=1>. [2013].

2. BMC Software, *Discover and dynamically track your IT hardware and software assets.* Available from: <http://www.numarasoftware. com/footprints/inventorymanagement/>.[2013].

3. Eubanks, R., *The SANS Institute, A Small Business No Budget Implementation of the SANS 20 Security Controls.* Available from: <http:// cse.spsu.edu/raustin2/coursefiles/id/SmallBusNoBudgetImplSans-20SecControls.pdf>.[10 Aug 2011].

www.ingramcontent.com/pod-product-compliance
Lightning Source LLC
Chambersburg PA
CBHW070041210526
45170CB00012B/563